Oxford Guide to Plain English

SECOND EDITION

Martin Cutts

OXFORD
UNIVERSITY PRESS

OXFORD
UNIVERSITY PRESS

Great Clarendon Street, Oxford OX2 6DP

Oxford University Press is a department of the University of Oxford.
It furthers the University's objective of excellence in research, scholarship,
and education by publishing worldwide in

Oxford New York

Auckland Bangkok Buenos Aires Cape Town Chennai Dar es Salaam
Delhi Florence Hong Kong Istanbul Karachi Kolkata Kuala Lumpur
Madrid Melbourne Mexico City Mumbai Nairobi Shanghai São Paulo
Taipei Tokyo Toronto

Oxford is a registered trade mark of Oxford University Press
in the UK and in certain other countries

Published in the United States
by Oxford University Press Inc., New York

Database right Oxford University Press (maker)

First published as The Plain English Guide 1996
Published as the Quick Reference Plain English Guide 1999
This edition published 2004

British Library Cataloguing in Publication Data
Data available

Library of Congress Cataloging in Publication Data

Data available

ISBN 0–19–861011–4

10 9 8 7 6 5 4 3 2 1

Printed in the UK by Ashford Colour Press Ltd, Gosport, Hampshire

Contents

TO IVOR AND JOAN CUTTS
for all their support and encouragement

Acknowledgements

My thanks go to those who commented on the manuscript: Nick Moore, Katie Shipsides, Tony Mercer, Ivor Cutts and Kevin Cutts. Throughout the writing of the book, my wife gave constant help and support. I am also grateful to Monica Sowash, who conducted the focus group interviews.

Extracts from a debt advice booklet in chapter 21 are reproduced by permission of The Birmingham Settlement National Debtline, the copyright owners.

The author is the research director of Plain Language Commission.

Starting points

The postman arrives, bringing a slip of paper from an insurance company. No surprise in that, as I'm expecting an acknowledgement of a payment I've sent them. The surprise is that it's written like this:

The said aggregate further single premium shall be apportioned equally among the existing Policies and consequently in relation to each such Policy the Further Minimum Sum Assured secured by the part of the said aggregate further single premium apportioned thereto shall be a sum equal to the aggregate Further Minimum Sum Assured specified in the Schedule divided by the total number of the existing Policies the Further Participating Sum Assured so secured shall be a sum equal to the aggregate Further Participating Sum Assured so specified divided by the total number of the existing Policies and the amount of the further single premium paid under each of the existing Policies shall be a sum equal to the further aggregate single premium so specified divided by the total number of the existing Policies

Signed by the company's president and by its managing director, this is a single unpunctuated sentence of 132 words – not even a full stop at the end. A strange way indeed of keeping the customers happy and encouraging them to send more money.

The mail also includes a letter from the manager of the city post office. It begins:

I again return your application for renewal of road fund licence and reitterate the correct is amount is £130.

I have enclosed a photocopy of your original envelope you will notice it it clearly datestamped 2nd December, some two days after Budget day.

To make four errors in 43 words doesn't prove the organization is about to collapse, but gives an impression of incompetence.

Customers could be forgiven for suspecting the judgement of any writer so careless.

There's also a letter from a college's 'Director of Quality' to a student who has had the temerity to use the 'Student Grievance Procedure'. Part of it goes:

> From the plethora of letters that have been received from you [...] it is impossible to determine the gravamen of your complaint.

The student asks me whether this kind of language – along with 'preliminary procedural representations', 'preliminary representations on points of procedure' and 'preliminary representations' – is acceptable: 'My opinion,' he says, 'is that he is deliberately trying to confuse me.' Battered by these examples, I seek solace in a train journey to Blaenau Ffestiniog in North Wales, only to find this sentence in a printed notice near the flush toilet:

> Failure to observe the above instructions will result in the malfunction of this ammenity [sic].

This book is about those four pieces of writing and about the millions of others – many of them, thankfully, much more lucid and well expressed – that are produced every day at work.

The book is not about the writing of novels, plays, poetry or newspapers. It focuses on 'essential information', a loose description that includes business and government letters and reports; consumer contracts; product instructions; leaflets and forms on tax, health, welfare and legal rights; and rules, regulations and laws. These things may seem humdrum compared to the mighty works of literature, but they help to oil the engines of industry, commerce and administration. They provide information which, if misunderstood or half understood, disadvantages people, oppresses them or – at the least – wastes their time and money. It is important to write these documents well.

Guidance not rules

The book has one main aim: to help you write and set out essential information clearly. It does this by suggesting and examining 21 guidelines often used by professional editors.

I say guidelines, not rules. There is a guideline to aim for an average sentence length of 15–20 words in a document, but there is no rule prohibiting sentences of more than 20 words. There is a guideline to use words your readers are likely to understand, but there is no rule prohibiting technical terms.

So this is not meant to be a simple recipe book or a set of quick fixes. Writing will still be hard work – perhaps the hardest work you do – but the guidelines should make it easier and help you produce results that are more readily understood.

The examples used in the book are authentic apart from some of the obvious fictions I have created in chapter 15. I have changed words only to protect authors' anonymity or to add enough context to help you make sense of the examples.

For some of the examples, I have provided rewrites. These are not meant to be the sole or perfect solutions. There are many ways of saying the same thing; if you can improve on my versions, so much the better.

No writing can truly be regarded as clearer or better, however, until users' performance proves it. Several times I mention the value of testing high-use documents with likely users, to see whether they can follow the information and act upon it. I have taken my own advice by testing the clarity of some of the pairs of 'before' and 'after' examples shown. A focus group of 35 people rated the examples for clarity by giving them a score out of 20. The focus group included police officers, firefighters, library staff, unemployed people, teachers, pensioners, booksellers, gardeners – and one person who described herself as a dogsbody. Though focus groups are not statistically representative of the population, they give a useful snapshot of readers' perceptions.

In general, the focus group preferred the versions that heeded the guidelines, rating them significantly clearer than the originals. This does not prove that the performance of group members in a real-life situation would have been better, but it is a strong indicator. The results, shown at appropriate points in the text, enable me to recommend the guidelines to you with even greater confidence.

What is plain English?

The guidelines will help you create plain-English documents. But what is really meant by plain English? Is it anything more than a slogan used by campaigners to publicize themselves and their favourite cause, and by businesses selling editing and document design services?

Undoubtedly, plain English is a woolly term. As no formula can genuinely measure the plainness of a document, I would rather describe plain English than define it. In my view, plain English refers to:

The writing and setting out of essential information in a way that gives a co-operative, motivated person a good chance of understanding it at first reading, and in the same sense that the writer meant it to be understood.

This means pitching the language at a level of sophistication that suits the readers and using appropriate structure and layout to help them navigate through the document. It does not mean always using simple words at the expense of the most accurate words or writing whole documents in kindergarten language – even if, as some adult literacy surveys claim, about seven million adults in the UK and 70 million adults in the US cannot read and write competently.

As well as its strong connotations of clarity, 'plainness' is about honesty. Essential information should not lie or tell half-truths, especially as its providers are often socially or financially dominant. For example, insurance and pension companies should not hide their charges beneath a mass of detail and doublespeak. A health advisory booklet should not withhold facts that political, religious or minority groups might find unpalatable. Products claiming green credentials should not use duplicitous labels like 'recyclable', since almost anything can be recycled, or 'harvested from sustainable forests', since all forests are sustainable and what matters is whether they are indeed sustained, and how.

Plain English is not an absolute: what is plain to an audience of scientists or philosophers may be obscure to everyone else. And because of variations in usage across the English-speaking world, what is plain in Manchester may be obscure in Madras or Maine. Similarly, what is plain today may be obscure a hundred years from now because patterns of usage, readers' prior knowledge and readers' expectations will all alter over time.

The book concentrates on the written word, though of course users of the spoken word can get themselves in a tangle when under pressure to fill a silence. Having partly disrobed the pop singer Janet Jackson during a live concert on US nationwide television in 2004, exposing her star-encrusted nipple, Justin Timberlake called the whole thing a 'wardrobe malfunction'. In 2003 US defense secretary Donald Rumsfeld made himself seem even more cerebral than usual by declaring:

> **Reports that say that something hasn't happened are always interesting to me, because as we know, there are known knowns; there are things we know we know. We also know there are known unknowns; that is to say we know there are some things we do not know. But there are also unknown unknowns – the ones we don't know we don't know.**

Where did plain English spring from?

Pleas for plain English have been around for a long time. In the fourteenth century Chaucer had one of his characters demand:

> **Speketh so pleyne at this time, I yow preye**
> **That we may understonde what ye seye.**

In 1500, *Chaucer's Dreme* refers to a story 'which ye shalle here in pleyne Englische'. The few remaining writings of William Tyndale do not reveal whether he saw himself as plain Englishing the Latin Bible in 1525. But his influential translation, for which he was executed, certainly used the direct and pungent voice of the common people of his day. And Tyndale seems to have been keen on the modern plain-English principle of keeping the readers in mind, if his growl to one opponent is anything to go by: 'If God spare my life, ere many years I will cause a boy that driveth the plough shall know more of the scripture than thou dost.'

In 1550, after only three years on the throne of England, Edward VI had become so exasperated with the law that he remarked:

I would wish that the superfluous and tedious statutes were made more plain and short, to the intent that men might better understand them.

Regrettably he didn't reign long enough to do much about it.

In the same century some writers wanted to halt the influx of what they called inkhorn terms such as 'revoluting', 'ingent affabilitie' and 'magnifical dexteritie', which were meant to broaden what could be said in English and make it sound more grand. Some inkhorn terms like 'defunct' and 'inflate' survive to this day as plain words because people have found them useful.

In 1604 Robert Cawdray's first-ever English-to-English dictionary sought to explain:

hard vsuall English wordes, borrowed from the Hebrew, Greeke, Latine, or French. &c. With the interpretation thereof by plaine English words, gathered for the benefit & helpe of Ladies, Gentlewomen, or any other vnskilfull persons.

Patronizing though that seems today, this dictionary of barely 2,000 entries was meant to help people whose lack of access to private tutors and grammar schools left them unable to understand the heavily latinized English that was then so fashionable among the high and powerful.

From the seventeenth century, Protestants, especially Quakers, tended to favour a simple style in their writing and speaking. They called it plain language. In nineteenth-century England, others sought a weird kind of linguistic purity by trying to replace Latin-derived words with those of a Saxon look. William Barnes, for example, preferred 'leechcraft' to 'medicine', 'speechlore' to 'grammar', and 'swanling' to 'cygnet'. His terms 'foreword' (instead of 'preface') and 'handbook' (instead of 'manual') are today as popular as their alternatives. The English barrister George Coode began trying to get legal sentences written more clearly. He said, rather too optimistically:

Nothing more is required than that instead of an accidental and incongruous style, the common popular structure of plain English be resorted to.

The philosopher Jeremy Bentham called for laws to be divided up into sections (this was being done in France), demanded shorter sentences (one law included a 13-page sentence) and suggested that lawyers should 'speak intelligibly to whom you speak'.

In England in the 1920s, C K Ogden and I A Richards devised Basic English. Its core was a vocabulary of 850 words which, in various combinations and using a narrow range of sentence structures, could, they believed, say everything that needed to be said. Their three aims were that Basic should be an international language, an introduction to full standard English for foreigners, and a kind of plain language for use in science, commerce and government. Basic was supported by Winston Churchill, the British prime minister, and by Franklin Roosevelt, the US president. Though influential to this day in the teaching of English as a foreign language, Basic became bogged down in academic controversy and eventually fizzled out as a force for plain language in the 1950s.

In that decade a landmark for plain English was erected when the British government's Treasury commissioned Ernest Gowers, a top civil servant, to write a book encouraging plain writing in the civil service and elsewhere. This eventually became *The Complete Plain Words*, still widely read in updated editions. Unfortunately the book continues to exempt many forms of legal drafting from its advice, a loophole that some lawyers have pleaded in mitigation of their often wayward writing habits.

Modern developments

In the late 1960s and early 1970s the seeds of a modern plain-English revolution were sown. **In the US**, consumer groups used the mass media to publicize and ridicule examples of obscurity in legal documents and government forms, calling for plain language or plain English. In 1974 Siegel & Gale, a pioneering company in the document design field, worked with Citibank in New York to rewrite a loan agreement that customers and staff could understand. The Citibank loan note was so revolutionary it was publicized across America. At federal level, it led to the Magnuson–Moss Act requiring guarantees or warranties to be in plain language. At state level, it led to laws requiring leases and consumer contracts to be clear, first in New York State in 1978 and then in many others – to the dismay of some lawyers. That obscurity could also be politically oppressive had been shown in the sixties when the civil-rights movement challenged a Louisiana statute requiring black (African–American) people to interpret difficult passages from the constitution before they were allowed to vote. 'We hold,' said John Minor Wisdom, the judge, 'that this wall, built to bar negroes from access to the franchise, must come down.' In 1973 the American National Council of Teachers of English formed a Public Doublespeak Committee to draw attention to the use of deceptive language by public figures, and established a George Orwell Award for honesty and clarity in public language.

In 1978 President Carter signed executive order 12044 requiring regulations to be written in plain English. In 1998 President Clinton issued a memorandum, 'Plain Language in Government Writing', which said:

The Federal Government's writing must be in plain language. By using plain language, we send a clear message about what the Government is doing, what it requires, and what services it offers. Plain language saves the Government and the private sector time, effort and money.

Plain language requirements vary from one document to another, depending on the intended audience. Plain language documents have logical organization, easy-to-read design features, and use:

- **common, everyday words, except for necessary technical terms;**
- **"you" and other pronouns;**
- **the active voice; and**
- **short sentences.**

The memo then directs the heads of executive departments and agencies to use plain language from October 1998 in all new documents that explain how to get a benefit or service 'or how to comply with a regulation you administer or enforce'. Regulations were excepted from this, but Clinton also required that by January 1999 plain language be used 'in all proposed and final rulemakings published in the *Federal Register*' unless the rule was proposed before that date. Both the Carter and Clinton edicts ceased to be enforced when the presidency changed hands, but they were landmarks and their influence continues.

In 1998 the Securities and Exchange Commission (SEC) instructed corporations to write key parts of stock and bond prospectuses – especially the cover page, summary and risk factors – in plain language. Arthur Levitt Jr, SEC chairman, told Associated Press, 'I've been around our markets most of my life and I can't understand much of what passes for disclosure.'

To help corporations comply, the SEC website offered an excellent free guide to writing plain language in financial documents, the *Plain English Handbook* (www.sec.com). The foreword was by Warren Buffett, an investor with cult status in the US: 'When writing [my company's] annual report, I pretend that I'm talking to my sisters. I have no trouble picturing them: Though highly intelligent, they are not experts in accounting or finance. They will understand plain English, but jargon may puzzle them. My goal is simply to give them the information I would wish them to supply me if our positions were reversed. To succeed, I don't need to be Shakespeare; I must, though, have a sincere desire to inform.' Bell Atlantic was among the first companies to comply with the new rules. It showed what could be done with a merger document, being content to replace this:

> **In the Merger, each share of NYNEX Common Stock issued and outstanding immediately before the Effective Time (excluding those held in the treasury of NYNEX and those owned by Bell Atlantic) without action on the part of the holder thereof, will be converted into the right to receive 0.768 of a share of Bell Atlantic Common Stock.**

with this:

> **If the merger is completed, Nynex stockholders will receive 0.768 of a share of Bell Atlantic common stock for each share of Nynex common stock that they own.**

The importance of thinking carefully about an audience's needs and, ideally, testing the usability of key public documents with them was evident in the muddle over the presidential elections in 2000. In Palm Beach County, the election supervisor decided that with 10 names to fit on the ballot paper, two pages would be better than one. This, she felt, would make it easier for a mainly elderly electorate to deal with. She got the design of the paper approved by all the parties and the authorities. Yet when the real target audience came to use the paper, the design so misled them that 19,000 people double-punched their papers, invalidating them, while many staunch Democrats voted mistakenly for a right-wing candidate. From the ensuing mayhem, George W Bush emerged victorious over his Democrat rival, and many believe that world history has been significantly altered by a poor piece of document design.

In the UK there was even a whiff of book-burning in 1979 as campaigners for plain English, in a protest I organized, shredded unclear government forms outside the Houses of Parliament. This struck such a chord with the incoming Thatcher government that in 1982 it issued a White Paper (a policy statement) ordering departments for the first time to count their forms, abolish unnecessary ones, clarify the rest, and report their progress annually to the prime minister. As Mrs Thatcher actually read the reports and held senior officials to account, this meant something. By the end of the 1980s, under her onslaught, it was difficult to find a truly atrocious central government form in the UK. Local government has also been influenced. Some town halls have set up plain-English committees of elected members and officials who vet forms and leaflets for clarity before they are printed. One puts a logo on its approved documents saying 'Plain English by Derby City Council'. Similar accreditation schemes are also sold commercially. Two of the best known are run by Plain Language Commission (from 1994) and Plain English Campaign Ltd (from 1990). In both cases documents meeting the scheme criteria may display the respective logos, further publicizing the accreditation and attracting new customers. In response to widespread mistrust and incomprehension of such products as pensions, a scheme for the financial services sector has been run by the Pensions Protection Investments Accreditation Board since 2001, supported by subscriptions from the brands it certifies as 'tested for clarity, quality, service'. A fourth scheme, from the Centre for Health Information Quality (established by the National Health Service Executive), has accredited the clarity and accuracy of public health information since 2001.

Often it is only when things go wrong that people look at the small print of their insurance contracts and the like. When a House of Lords ruling in 2000 revealed a £1.5bn ($2bn) hole in the finances of the mutual insurer Equitable Life, customers rushed to their policies to see when they could extract their money on the most favourable terms. There they found language that wouldn't have been out of place in the year of Equitable's foundation, 1762. There were sentences of 125, 159 and even 218 words, and this relative minnow of 62 words:

Notwithstanding anything hereinbefore contained no partial surrender may be effected unless both the sum payable on the partial surrender and the total after the surrender of the Participating Sum Assured and the Related Bonuses thereon and of all Further Participating Sums Assured and Related Bonuses thereon exceed a minimum sum which the Society shall determine at the time of the partial surrender.

A sentence need not be long for it to baffle people unused to high-level language. After a government agency wrote 'This charter is neither extensive nor exhaustive', an informal survey found that many of the target audience confused 'extensive' with 'expensive', and 'exhaustive' with 'exhausting', thus interpreting the sentence as 'This charter is neither costly nor tiring.' The original made better sense when rewritten as 'This charter does not try to give you every detail.'

One bus-driver in Derbyshire took matters into his own hands when confronted by a bemusing company textbook. He got national publicity in 2001 after translating its 183 rules into readable prose, much of which was adopted by the firm. Instead of 'Ensure the potential impact of non-routine factors and problems and other services are assessed and details notified promptly to an appropriate person', he wrote 'Inform the depot if you are stuck in traffic or involved in an accident.' Instead of 'Ensure machinery for issuing and endorsing tickets is confirmed as in working order and is set in accordance with approved procedure', he wrote 'Check the ticket machine is showing the correct date and price.'

Plain English has the best chance of flourishing when government opts for simplicity in its regulations and schemes. Housing benefit forms that seemed long at four or six pages in the 1980s are now routinely 12- and 16-page monsters. The questions may be reasonably clear, but there are hundreds of them. Similarly, in the area of tax-free savings, the abolition in 1999 of the easy-to-understand personal equity plans and tax-exempt special savings accounts in favour of individual savings accounts (ISAs) spawned a new wave of incomprehension among consumers that will persist until at least 2009 when ISAs are reviewed.

Of course, there is plenty of good, clear writing around. Even humble carrier bags from the successful sandwich chain Pret A Manger have a well-written marketing message:

> **Every Pret has its own kitchen. We don't have a factory. We make our sandwiches, baguettes and PretWraps one by one, right here, throughout the day. You won't find sell-by dates and storage information on our sandwiches and wraps. If our fresh food doesn't sell out each day we give it away to charity rather than compromise our standards.**

And several government documents are clearly outstanding examples of plain language. For instance the Health and Safety Executive's *Health and Safety at Motor Sports Events* is a thing of beauty – lively writing, attractive page layouts, pleasing type and good photos. Even for those who find motor-sport unappealing, the booklet is a real page-turner.

The first use of the phrase 'plain English' in British law seems to have been in the 1974 Consumer Credit Act, when credit reference agencies were required to give consumers, on request, the contents of their file 'in plain English'. So if companies were using code or some other abbreviated form, they had to convert the file into language that the ordinary person could readily understand.

European law has given a powerful boost to the use of plain language in certain standard-form consumer contracts. EC Council directive 93/13 requires unfair terms to be removed, and:

> **In the case of contracts where all or certain terms offered to the consumer are in writing, these terms must always be drafted in plain, intelligible language. Where there is doubt about the meaning of a term, the interpretation most favourable to the consumer shall prevail.**

The Office of Fair Trading (OFT) is one of the main enforcers in the UK of regulation 7 of the Unfair Terms in Contracts Regulations 1999, which, in line with the directive, requires many of the terms of consumer contracts to be written in plain and intelligible language. 'A term is open to challenge as unfair,' says the OFT, 'if it could put the consumer at a disadvantage because he or she is not clear about

its meaning – even if its meaning could be worked out by a lawyer.'
Even the core terms – those setting out the price or defining the
product – must comply with the plain-language rule otherwise they
can be subject to a test of fairness, making this a powerful incentive
for firms to clear up their core terms. The OFT also says that 'jargon-
free language is of no value to consumers unless it is in legible print',
and has used its powers to ensure that print is big enough to read.
This affects, for example, car-hire contracts, which are often in such
tiny type that they are virtually indecipherable without a magnifying
glass. The OFT publishes a quarterly bulletin (www.oft.gov.uk) of
case reports on the hundreds of contract terms it has ordered to be
rewritten or deleted. Bulletins 23–25 (2003) are particularly tough
on legal expressions like indemnify; principals; shall vest in the pupil;
tenants in common; joint and several liability; right of appropriation;
we shall lay blameless; herein; lien; reversion; long term reduced payment moratorium; forthwith; time is of the essence; without
prejudice; *mutatis mutandis*; void or voidable; successors in title;
demises; undertake; and condition precedent.

Often an OFT challenge results in whole clauses being deleted
because they are unnecessary, meaningless or unlawful. In one case,
a property business withdrew its entire tenancy agreement of 41
clauses and replaced it with model terms from a trade association,
while Bradford and Bingley plc withdrew a 59-clause agreement
after its clarity was challenged.

In 1995 the government set up the Tax Law Rewrite Project to
convert tax law into plainer English. The project began with a staff
of 40 (including law drafters from the government's parliamentary
counsel's office), an annual budget of £2.5m ($4.5m), and 6,000
pages of tax law to redraft. Chunks of the rewritten tax law are now
in force, and there is also a new, clearer page layout for all laws.
Some new laws read as if they have been heavily influenced by
plain-language thinking. The Elections Act 2001, the Human Rights
Act 1998, the Land Registration Act 2002 and the Arbitration Act
1996 all make good use of short sentences, well-constructed vertical
lists and (in the case of the Elections Act) headings positioned in the
main column of the page not as sidenotes. There is still much to do:
one transposition of a European Commission (EC) directive into

British law includes a 202-word sentence, even though the original EC text was fairly straightforward. This kind of complexity imposes a heavy cost on those who must comply.

Much depends on who is thought to be the audience for legislation. I believe legislators should regard their primary audience as interested private citizens, not lawyers. Laws may never be written in the plainest of plain language, but they should at least be understandable to reasonably literate, motivated people who are prepared to make an effort. It may be a pretty big effort, of course, especially in technical areas of law. Yet many non-lawyers must from time to time read laws in their raw state – police officers, local authority officials, tax collectors, special interest groups, trade unionists, and that very special group of ordinary citizens who happen – usually without the benefit of any training in the law – to have been elected as members of the various UK parliaments. Focusing on their needs would help to clarify the law for all, including lawyers.

In Australia during the 1970s the first car insurance policy that could reasonably be called 'plain' was issued, and the example was widely copied and refined in that country and the UK. In 1984 the Australian government adopted a plain-language policy for its public documents and this is being extended to the language of the law itself. Law-writers in Canberra now take advice from their own *Plain English Manual*. In Queensland the Industrial Relations Reform Bill 1993 even legislates for clarity – tribunal decisions must be 'expressed in plain English' and 'structured in a way that is as easy to understand as the subject matter allows'. There is a political push behind this. Politicians not only scent a vote or two in plain English, as it removes another remnant of Australia's colonial past, but see it as a way of cutting the cost of government and compliance with regulations.

There are also plain-language movements at different stages of development in **Canada, Sweden, Italy, Germany** and **France**. Advocates of plain Swedish have exerted considerable influence over the language of new laws for many years. No government bill, including proposed acts of Parliament, can go to the printers without the approval of the ministry of justice's 'division for legal and linguistic draft revision'. In 2000 the division revised 1,187 acts, 1,959 ordinances and 110 committee terms of reference.

Does plain English work?

Research shows that documents carefully crafted in plain English can improve readers' comprehension. In an American study of instructions given by word of mouth to jurors, the plain versions improved comprehension by 14 percentage points, from 45 per cent to 59 per cent. In a further study the same instructions were given in both speech and writing. Jurors understood the plain versions 'almost fully', said the researchers. In a study to test understanding of medical consent forms in the US, readers of the original form could answer correctly only 2.36 questions out of 5. Using the plainer form they got 4.52 questions right, a 91 per cent improvement; they also took much less time to answer. In 1999 the Social Security Administration (SSA) wanted to issue an annual benefit statement to every working American over 25 years old, some 125 million people. Plain-language experts at the Center for Clear Communication, Inc tested the previous six-page form and found it poorly structured and presented, with some important details buried. So they wrote, designed and pilot-tested four prototypes of a new form. These versions had a clear title, good organization and a design that reduced production and handling costs. They were consumer-tested through a national mail survey of 16,000 people. A Gallup survey in 2000 reported that '…the results to date are glowing. The new social security statements have played a significant role in increasing Americans' understanding of social security'.

In the UK, Plain Language Commission tested my Clearer Timeshare Act (a law rewritten in plain English) with 90 senior law students in 1994. Nine out of 10 preferred the plain version to the real act. Performance also improved: on one key question, 94 per cent got the correct answer when working with the rewritten version, while only 48 per cent did so with the real act.

My pretend law was never meant to become the real thing, but it had an immediate effect. Two groups of tax and accountancy professionals were formed to persuade the Inland Revenue (the UK tax department) to rewrite tax laws into plainer English. I helped one of them translate a tax law into modern English from the original gobbledygook agreed by Parliament. Surprisingly, the government's own law drafters in the parliamentary counsel's office did the same kind of thing, effectively rewriting a chunk of their own work and proposing it to the Revenue. The result of all this was the Tax Law Rewrite Project referred to above. So pressure for change paid off, and the reforms arising from that project have been widely welcomed in the tax and accountancy fields.

Much of the most convincing research on the benefits of plain English relates to legal documents. And the most telling point of all is that no company that has issued a plain-English insurance policy, pension contract or bank guarantee has ever reverted to a traditional, legalistic style of wording.

The point of plain English

What has motivated me and many others to work for the plain-English cause is that clearer documents can improve people's access to services, benefits, justice and a fair deal. If people understand what they are asked to read and sign, they can make more informed choices and know more about their rights and duties. They might even see more clearly what business and government are up to, just as US freedom-of-information laws have enabled people to discover what is being done in their name. Plain language should, I believe, become an accepted part of plain dealing between consumers and business, and between citizens and the State. I hope this book will help it to do so.

Summary of guidelines

Most of the chapters begin with a guideline that is then expanded and discussed. The 21 guidelines are set out below. Numbers correspond to chapter numbers.

Style and grammar

1 Over the whole document, make the average sentence length 15–20 words.

2 Use words your readers are likely to understand.

3 Use only as many words as you really need.

4 Prefer the active voice unless there's a good reason for using the passive.

5 Use clear, crisp, lively verbs to express the actions in your document.

6 Use vertical lists to break up complicated text.

7 Put your points positively when you can.

8 Reduce cross-references to a minimum.

9 Try to avoid sexist usage.

10 In letters, avoid fusty first sentences and formula finishes.

11 Put accurate punctuation at the heart of your writing.

12 Avoid being enslaved by writing myths.

13 You can be a good writer without learning hundreds of grammatical terms.

Preparing and planning

14 Plan before you write.

Organizing the information

15   Organize your material in a way that helps readers to grasp the important information early and to navigate through the document easily.

16   Consider different ways of setting out your information.

Management of writing

17   Manage colleagues' writing carefully and considerately to boost their morale and effectiveness.

Plain English for specific purposes: e-mails, instructions and legal documents

18   Take as much care with e-mail as you would with the rest of your writing.

19   Devote special effort to producing lucid and well-organized instructions.

20   Apply plain-English techniques to legal documents such as insurance policies, car-hire agreements, laws and wills.

Layout

21   Use clear layout to present your plain words in an easily accessible way.

1 | Writing shorter sentences . . . or chopping up snakes

Guideline: *Over the whole document, make the average sentence length 15–20 words.*

More people fear snakes than full stops, so they recoil when a long sentence comes hissing across the page. Here's one from an accountant's letter to his self-employed client:

> Our annual bill for services (which unfortunately from your viewpoint has to increase to some degree in line with the rapid expansion of your business activities) in preparing the accounts and dealing with tax (please note there will be higher-rate tax assessments for us to deal with on this level of profit, which is the most advantageous time to invest in your personal pension fund, unless of course changes are made in the Chancellor's Budget Statement) and general matters arising, is enclosed herewith for your kind attention.

At one level, the sentence is easy to read – all the words are clear enough for a literate client. What makes it hard work is its length and muddle, with asides and additions tagged on as they sprang into the writer's mind.

Muddle is more likely in a long sentence unless the construction is simple and well organized. Instead of making one main point – and perhaps one related subsidiary point – a long sentence force-feeds the reader with point after point after point. This demands more concentration and short-term memory, leading to overload if the topic is complicated. If you want to get your recommendation agreed by a board of directors, it is unwise to waste their time disentangling a 68-word sentence like this:

> Although Mr Smith's requested increase in borrowing facility is substantial and the Smith Group has not yet returned to acceptable profitability, in fact because of dividends paid there was a deficit of £10 million transferred to revenue reserves, profits at the trading

**level have increased with considerable opportunity to advance
further as the recession eases and consumer confidence improves,
therefore an increased limit to £12.5 million is recommended.**

But what length of sentence is too long? Ignore advice that pre-
scribes an upper limit, though if you regularly exceed 40 words you
will certainly weary your readers. Better to aim for an average of
15–20 words throughout. The key word is *average*, so not all sentences need to be in this range; there should be plenty of variety.
While an occasional short sentence will punch home an important
point effectively, too many will make your writing dull and staccato.
There is no lower limit: a sentence could be just one word, such as
'Why?', or two words, such as 'I disagree' or 'Not so'.

One reason for keeping to a 15–20 word average is that people
are used to it. In the mid-1960s, a million words of published US
writing were analysed. The average sentence length was 19. Scores
for particular types of document included:

• Miscellaneous: government	25
• Learned and scientific	24
• Press: reviews	22
• Press: reports	21
• Humour	18
• Fiction: romance/love	14
• Fiction: science/detective	13

It's notable that government documents, perhaps the only material that could be classed as essential information, came top.

If you find yourself writing long sentences or having to edit them
for other people, there are six main ways of clarifying them:

- Split and disconnect.
- Split and connect.
- Say less.
- Use a list.
- Cut verbiage.
- Bin the sentence and start again.

Let's examine each of these.

Split and disconnect

Full stops enable readers to digest your latest point and prepare for the next. This sentence from a local government report makes good sense but, at 57 words, is too long for busy people to grasp at first reading:

> I understand that some doctors making night calls have been attacked in recent months on the expectation that they were carrying drugs and their caution when visiting certain areas in the south of the city has been very exacting and has even included telephoning the address to be visited from their car when they arrive outside the house.

Look for the main break in the sense. It comes in the second line after 'drugs', where the writer starts talking about caution. So you could split it there, delete 'and', and produce this:

> I understand that some doctors making night calls have been attacked in recent months on the expectation that they were carrying drugs. Their caution when visiting certain areas in the south of the city has been very exacting and has even included telephoning the address to be visited from their car when they arrive outside the house.

That may be enough. But you could go further and split it again after 'exacting', producing this:

> I understand that some doctors making night calls have been attacked in recent months on the expectation that they were carrying drugs. Their caution when visiting certain areas in the south of the city has been very exacting. It has even included telephoning the address to be visited from their car when they arrive outside the house.

Now the paragraph can be readily grasped at first reading, though you could go further and express the ideas more smoothly:

> Recently, some doctors making night calls have been attacked because they were thought to be carrying drugs. So they have started to take stringent precautions when visiting the south of the city. These have even included phoning the patient's home from their car on arrival.

Split and connect

This means putting in a full stop and restarting the sentence with a connecting word like 'however', 'but', 'so', 'also', 'yet' or 'further'. The technique would be helpful in this example from a lawyer's letter:

Whilst it is expected by the donor's family that the present arrangement for caring for the donor will continue for the rest of her life, should it at any stage become necessary to transfer the donor once more into a nursing institution, the donor's family envisages that the second-floor flat will be sold and the donor's share in the proceeds used to provide any additional income necessary to ensure her continued well-being.

That's a 73-word sentence – not enormous, perhaps, but certainly a candidate for splitting. The obvious break point is after 'life' in the third line:

Whilst it is expected by the donor's family that the present arrangement for caring for the donor will continue for the rest of her life.

But this fails because the sentence is unfinished – nothing complete has yet been said. Striking out 'Whilst', however, creates a complete sentence and the next can begin with 'but' (see chapter 12 if that worries you):

~~Whilst~~ **It is expected by the donor's family that the present arrangement for caring for the donor will continue for the rest of her life. But should it at any stage become necessary to transfer the donor once more into a nursing institution, the donor's family envisages that the second-floor flat will be sold and the donor's share in the proceeds used to provide any additional income necessary to ensure her continued well-being.**

Other improvements are possible. At the start, it would be simpler to say 'The donor's family expects . . .'. The second sentence could be full-stopped at 'sold', with a new one beginning 'The donor's share in the proceeds would then be used . . .'.

Say less

Sometimes a sentence is lengthened by needless repetition, as at the start of this lawyer's letter:

Dear Sirs
Trial of John Smith and James Jackson
Trade Descriptions Act 1968, Manchester Crown Court, 10.30 am, Tuesday 7 June 2000
The above defendants are to be tried at the Manchester Crown Court on Tuesday 7 June 2000 at 10.30 am for several offences under the

Trade Descriptions Act 1968 concerning the supply of motor vehicles
to which false trade descriptions had been applied.

As the first sentence repeats most of the heading, it could say:

Dear Sirs
<u>Trial of John Smith and James Jackson</u>
<u>Trade Descriptions Act 1968, Manchester Crown Court, 10.30 am,</u>
<u>Tuesday 7 June 2000</u>
The above defendants are to be tried for several offences concerning
the supply of motor vehicles to which false trade descriptions had
been applied.

That saves 18 words and preserves the meaning. It also lets the
heading do its job.

Use a list

Vertical lists break long sentences into manageable chunks. They
are particularly useful when describing a procedure, as in this safety
message to hospital staff about a machine for keeping babies warm:

The attachment of the warmer support-bearing assembly system
must be checked to ensure that it is adequately lubricated, its
securing screws are tight and that the warmer head can be easily
repositioned without the support bearing sticking.

Not a hard sentence for people in the trade – and only 38 words
long – but easier to follow in a vertical list with 'you' at the start to
make it more direct:

You must check the attachment of the warmer support-bearing
assembly system to ensure that:

(a)   it is adequately lubricated;
(b)   its securing screws are tight;
(c)   the warmer head can be easily repositioned without the
        support bearing sticking.

There's more on lists in chapter 6.

Cut verbiage

Sometimes the key ideas in a long sentence are buried under
verbiage:

The organizers of the event should try to achieve greater safety both
from the point of view of ensuring that the bonfire itself does not

**contain any unacceptably dangerous materials such as aerosol cans
or discarded foam furniture and from the point of view of ensuring
the letting-off of fireworks in the designated area, with easily
identifiable wardens to be available during the event to prevent
people indiscriminately letting off fireworks, to the possible danger
of people attending the event.**

The redundant words include 'from the point of view of' (twice),
'itself', 'unacceptably' (what are 'acceptably' dangerous materials?),
'discarded' (they wouldn't be on the bonfire otherwise), 'during the
event' and 'to the possible danger of people attending the event'
(redundant because crowd safety is what the whole sentence is
about). With verbiage crossed through and insertions underlined,
the sentence could be:

**The organizers of the event should try to achieve greater safety ~~both~~
<u>by</u> ~~from the point of view of~~ ensuring that the bonfire ~~itself~~ does not
contain any ~~unacceptably~~ dangerous materials such as aerosol cans
or ~~discarded~~ foam furniture and ~~from the point of view of~~ <u>by</u>
ensuring the letting-off of fireworks in the designated area, with
easily identifiable wardens to be available during the event to
prevent people indiscriminately letting off fireworks~~, to the possible
danger of people attending the event~~.**

Then, with a few minor modifications and a full stop after 'area',
the sentence becomes:

**The organizers of the event should try to achieve greater safety by
ensuring that the bonfire does not contain any dangerous materials
such as aerosol cans or foam furniture, and that fireworks are let off
only in the designated area. Easily identifiable wardens should be
present to prevent people letting off fireworks indiscriminately.**

And it could also be converted into a list, using the first 'that' as
a pivot and deleting the second 'that':

**The organizers of the event should try to achieve greater safety by
ensuring that:**

- **the bonfire does not contain any dangerous materials such
  as aerosol cans or foam furniture;**
- **fireworks are let off only in the designated area;**
- **easily identifiable wardens are present to stop people letting
  off their own fireworks.**

There's more on cutting verbiage in chapter 3.

Bin the sentence and start again

When there's no hope of untangling a sentence by other means, all you can do is discard it and rewrite. Here is that accountant's sentence from the top of the chapter, sadly unimproved since we left it:

> 1/ Our annual bill for services (which unfortunately from your viewpoint has to increase to some degree in line with the rapid expansion of your business activities) in preparing the accounts and dealing with tax (please note there will be higher-rate tax assessments for us to deal with on this level of profit, which is the most advantageous time to invest in your personal pension fund, unless of course changes are made in the Chancellor's Budget Statement) and general matters arising, is enclosed herewith for your kind attention.

It's no good just inserting full stops because the new sentences won't make any sense, and using a vertical list doesn't seem feasible. Nor does it help to make fewer points – it's all useful detail, though verbiage like 'from your viewpoint', 'general matters arising', 'herewith' and 'kind' could all be cut. So we need to start again and plan out the main points, which are:

(a) Here is our annual bill for services.
(b) We're charging more than last year for two reasons: your business has grown rapidly, and we'll have to work out a higher-rate tax assessment as you've made a lot more profit.
(c) Now is a good time to pay into your pension fund as you'll get higher-rate tax relief on your contributions, unless the rules alter in the Chancellor's budget.

This isn't the best sequence of points – the good news ought to come first. So, with the points in c-a-b order and written as sentences, the result could be:

> 2/ Now is a good time for you to pay into your pension fund as you will get higher-rate tax relief on your contributions – unless the Chancellor's budget changes the rules.
>
> I have enclosed our annual bill for services. Unfortunately it is higher than last year. This is because your business has grown rapidly and, since your profits are much greater, I will need to calculate a higher-rate tax assessment.

Four sentences – and readily understood at first reading. If you prefer a more informal style, you could put in some contractions (such as *I've, You'll*):

3/ Now is a good time for you to pay into your pension fund as you'll get higher-rate tax relief on your contributions – unless the Chancellor's budget changes the rules.

I've enclosed our annual bill for services. Unfortunately it's higher than last year. This is because your business has grown rapidly and, since your profits are much greater, I'll need to calculate a higher-rate tax assessment.

The last paragraph could also be written as a vertical list:

4/ Now is a good time for you to pay into your pension fund as you'll get higher-rate tax relief on your contributions – unless the Chancellor's budget changes the rules.

I have enclosed our annual bill for services. Unfortunately it is higher than last year. This is because:

- **your business has grown rapidly; and**
- **I will have to work out a higher-rate tax assessment as your profits are much greater.**

A 35-strong focus group (see page 3) assessed three of the four versions for clarity. They rated Version 4 the clearest, with an average score of 18 points from a possible 20. It was the first preference of 26 people. Version 2 got an average score of 14 but only three first preferences. Version 1, the original, scored only 5 points – seven respondents gave it no points at all. These results suggest that sentence length and layout significantly affect readers' perception of clarity.

Why bother?

Few people would think any less of accountants who occasionally write a bad sentence; after all, they're mainly in the figures business. But as the focus group showed, people do notice the difference between an accountant who writes considerately and one who doesn't. To any professional, the esteem and confidence of customers are valuable assets. So, if only for commercial reasons, it is important to control sentence length carefully. Fortunately this is easily done.

2 | Preferring plain words

Guideline: *Use words your readers are likely to understand.*

Here is a US Secretary of State refusing an assistant's request for a pay rise:

> Because of the fluctuational predisposition of your position's productive capacity as juxtaposed to government standards, it would be momentarily injudicious to advocate an increment.

And here is a local government official in England being obstructive to citizens who wish to display posters in a public library:

> Your request raises a question as to the provenance and veraciousness of the material, and I must consider individually all posters of a polemic or disputatious nature.

Both sentences over-dress simple ideas in phrases designed to impress not inform. In forelock-tugging times, people might have been impressed. Now they smell pomposity, and dislike being forced to translate.

For business writers this may be costly. An accountancy firm wrote a business proposal in this kind of language:

> At present the recessionary cycle is aggravating volumes through your modern manufacturing and order processing environments which provide restricted opportunities for cost reduction through labour adjustments and will remain a key issue.

What they probably meant was:

> Output and orders have fallen because of the recession but there is little scope for reducing the workforce.

Whatever they meant, they baffled their audience and didn't win the business.

A selling point obscured by waffle is likely to be missed by the readers. An aeronautics firm wrote to a prospective customer:

> We would anticipate being able to optimize the engine design from an emissions point of view.

In such a haystack of verbiage, the needle of meaning was lost:

We can redesign the engine to reduce emissions.

The BBC, which is in the clear communications business if any-one is, operates under a royal charter of such baffling complexity that it won Plain Language Commission's 'Golden Rhubarb' trophy in 1996. Amid sentences of 141 and 210 words, the vocabulary is strange and obscure: *mutatis mutandis*; conveyance of signals serving for the impartation of any matter; whereas on divers dates; subject as hereinafter provided; the aggregate of moneys; residual part thereof; aforesaid objects; requisite for the proper performance and obser-vance of its functions; the concurrence of the Council; deemed to vitiate any proceedings; exemplification thereof; determination of the said term; and anywise notwithstanding. Responding to a com-plaint about the charter's lack of clarity, the minister for media and heritage said in 2004: 'Although the wording of the beginning and end of the Royal Charter is fixed, the only requirement for the text of the body is that it is legally sound. Within that framework, I will make sure that the points you raise – which I agree with – are taken into account when any new Charter and Agreement are being drafted.' The documents are to be renewed in 2006.

In 1995 the British government issued a booklet to every house-hold in Northern Ireland on its ideas for peace in the province. Four times the prime minister's foreword said that people should read, understand and comment on it as part of a public debate. Yet the booklet was largely incomprehensible, with an average sentence length of 35 words and vocabulary that included unicameral; *ultra vires*; *inter alia*; cognizant of either option and open to its democratic realization; embrace the totality of relationships; instrument for an intensification; designated functions; appropriate new provisions entrenched by Agreement; comprehensive political accommoda-tion; weighted majority; adumbrated; prejudicing workability; interlocking and mutually supportive institutions; and quantum of public expenditure. There was no glossary to explain 'unicameral' and 'weighted majority', which were fundamental to the proposals. A local TV company took soundings in Belfast's markets area and found only mystification. One shopper said, 'I would like somebody to explain it to us all in words that we can understand. I want plain

English. I want it set down in front of me so that I can understand it and I can go to my children and say, this is what's happening.'

Especially outmoded is the ceremonial language found in town-twinning proclamations – written by normally down-to-earth city governments – and in royal pronouncements such as this citation on the Queen's Award for Export Achievement:

XYZ Company Limited: Greetings! We being cognizant of the outstanding achievement of the said body as manifested in the furtherance and increase of the Export Trade of our United Kingdom of Great Britain and Northern Ireland, our Channel Islands and our Isle of Man and being desirous of showing Our Royal Favour do hereby confer upon it the Queen's Award for Export Achievement.

Monarchs, like captains of any great corporation, should demand that their staff put clear, if dignified, language into their mouths. Be eloquent, not grandiose.

As English-speaking countries become more informal, many official bodies have promised to use plain language in their dealings with the public. Sir Ernest Gowers' motto, 'Be short, be simple, be human', has begun to take root. When people expect plain words, they are even more surprised to get officialese.

Is there no place for unusual words?

The chief reason for writing at work is to give information in a way that's readily understood – to bridge the gap between what you know and what the reader knows. Generally, plain words do this best. If you want to say:

Before the court case started, the usher asked everyone for silence

those are the plain words you would use. You wouldn't make people struggle with:

Prior to the commencement of the court case, the usher requested all persons present to adopt a mantle of quietude.

Not that there is anything wrong with long or unusual words in the right place and for the right audience (and many long words aren't unusual – think of 'immediately' or 'disappointment'). Sometimes an unusual word is perfect for the job, expressing just what you want to say. Then you should use it and either give an explanation or trust the context to explain; you should not always hope that busy readers will be willing to consult a dictionary, even supposing they own one. In a technical document, there is a place for technical words, which will be plain enough to technical people. But while doctors might readily understand 'cardiac atheroma' and 'pulmonary oedema', a mass audience would get a clearer sense of the ailments if explanations were added – 'furring-up of the heart's arteries' and 'fluid in the lungs'. It is pointless to say that a person is exhibiting xanthochromia and diaphoresis if you can say he is yellow and sweating. Generally, therefore, the place for unusual words is in technical contexts or in literature and journalism, where readers are prepared to travel further with a writer's flight of fancy.

Sometimes highly educated writers are surprised that words they regard as ordinary are unknown to the person sitting next to them on the train. Take that example about displaying posters in the library:

Your request raises a question as to the provenance and veraciousness of the material, and I must consider individually all posters of a polemic or disputatious nature.

Of the hundreds of educated people I've shown it to during writing-skills courses, only a handful have known that 'provenance' means 'origin' or 'source'. That may be regrettable but it sends a message to anyone with a wide vocabulary: don't assume that others know all the words you do. A paediatrician in the UK who stated her profession on a plaque outside her house found that her doors and windows were daubed with anti-paedophile graffiti. The vandal clearly didn't know what a paediatrician was, and hadn't stopped to wonder why a paedophile would advertise the fact on her house. Similarly, *Personnel Today* (18 July 2000) reports that when a communications director said in an office memo that he favoured a 'pedagogic' approach during training programmes, he was told to be out of the building by lunchtime as the company did not tolerate 'paedophilic perverts'. After he successfully pleaded a defence based on the Concise Oxford dictionary, a directive was sent to the entire staff saying that only words to be found in the local news-paper would be allowed in all future memos – a solution that owed more to face-saving than common sense.

In the queue at a bank cash point I watched a young man trying to decide from his balance slip whether his account held enough money to permit a withdrawal. He read it out to his friend: '£50.23 CR', but neither of them could tell whether CR (short for 'credit') meant he owed money to the bank or vice versa. In the end, they decided he was in debt and left without withdrawing any cash. Wrong decision, of course, but understandable since if you get credit you are putting yourself in debt. Some UK banks now speak of 'payments' and 'receipts' not debits and credits. Writers who want to be readily understood have a very tough job: they have to guess what words or symbols the reader is likely to understand, and write accordingly.

A similar problem arises with a word favoured by lawyers: 'notwithstanding'. When testing people's comprehension of legal documents, I've found that few non-lawyers can explain it – even in context. Alternative plain words are available: 'despite', 'in spite of', 'however' or 'but' can all do the same job. 'Notwithstanding', like 'forsooth', 'peradventure' and 'verily', has virtually disappeared from everyday speech and writing. Removing it and other oddities from legal documents will benefit people, not hammer a nail in the coffin of mass literacy by reducing their exposure to unusual words.

We shouldn't worry if archaic words disappear from time to time. When people no longer understand a word, or if it is not doing a useful job, its day is done and other words will move in to fill the gap. This has happened throughout history. Once, it was considered correct to use 'ye' in such constructions as 'ye believe', 'ye said' and 'gather ye rosebuds while ye may'. If anyone used 'ye' like this today, we'd think they had stepped out of a time machine. 'You' has ousted its rival and we seem to be none the worse.

The scope for using plain words – and the opposite – is rich in English because we have so many words with the same or similar meanings ('synonyms'). For example, the cauldron that bubbled for centuries with bits of Latin, French, Old Norse and Old English threw up several synonyms for 'start' – 'begin', 'commence', 'initiate', 'institute' and 'originate'. There is room for all these words, but only 'start' and 'begin' are first choices in today's plain-English lexicon.

Let's look at two main ways of removing officialese and pompous language:

- Use simpler alternatives.
- Reconstruct the sentences.

Use simpler alternatives

In this section, for the sake of clarity, the officialese and the equivalent plain English are underlined.

A local government department is writing to a tenant who has fallen behind with her rent. In law, the authority doesn't have to rehouse tenants it regards as deliberately homeless:

In the event of your being evicted from your dwelling as a result of wilfully failing to pay your rent, the council may take the view that you have rendered yourself intentionally homeless and as such it would not be obliged to offer you alternative permanent housing.

Using plain words and splitting the sentence, this could become:

If you are evicted from your home because you deliberately fail to pay your rent, the council may decide that you have made yourself intentionally homeless. If this happens, the council does not need to offer you alternative permanent housing.

Our focus group found this version far clearer, with 31 out of 35 preferring it. They gave it an average clarity mark of 17 out of 20, as against 12 for the original (a remarkable show of tolerance).

A hospital wants to resolve the chaos in its car parks by charging parking fees:

If my proposals are accepted, the income from fees would ensure that car parking control could be effected without utilising monies that should be expended on health care.

This becomes:

If my proposals are accepted, the income from fees would ensure that car parking could be controlled without using money that should be spent on health care.

An official is writing to a citizen about a claim for housing benefit:

I am in receipt of information from the citizens advice bureau, which I believe is acting on your behalf, with regard to matters appertaining to your benefit claim. Will you please <u>furnish</u> the bureau with <u>particulars</u> of your savings.

This becomes:

I have <u>received</u> information from the citizens advice bureau, which I believe is acting on your behalf, <u>about</u> your benefit claim. Will you please <u>give</u> the bureau <u>details</u> of your savings.

A firm's conditions of service say:

Holidays will be taken by mutual agreement after the <u>exigencies</u> of the service have been considered.

This becomes:

Holidays will be taken by mutual agreement after the <u>needs</u> of the service have been considered.

Reconstruct the sentences

The technique is to spot the unusual word or phrase and use its plain meaning as an aid in revising the sentence.

A trade union writes to its members:

It behoves management to give details of the planned redundancies, and it is incumbent on all members to participate fully in this dispute.

Deleting the unusual words, this becomes:

Management should [or 'has a duty to'] give details of the planned redundancies, and all members should [or 'must'] participate fully in this dispute.

A treasurer's report explains how many errors are being made when handling payments:

An approximate frequency for the mistakes was given by Mrs Jones as ten a month.

This becomes:

Mrs Jones said there were about ten mistakes a month.

J Edgar Hoover, when head of the US Federal Bureau of Investigation, was worried about Picasso visiting the country (he was said to have left-wing leanings). Hoover wrote to a special agent in Paris:

In the event information concerning Picasso comes to your attention, it should be furnished to the Bureau in view of the possibility that he may attempt to come to the United States.

He might have said:

If you get any information about Picasso, please tell the Bureau in case he tries to visit the US.

A company training officer is explaining a trend towards computer-based training:

The ready availability of computer-based tutorials associated with applications software has become prevalent since the development of Microsoft Windows.

To a fellow professional, none of these words would be hard to understand. But look closely at what is being said: 'The ready availability . . . has become prevalent'. Since 'ready availability' and 'prevalence' are so similar in meaning, the writer was probably trying to say:

Computer-based tutorials associated with applications software have become readily available since the development of Microsoft Windows.

Plain words make the meaning clearer and the sentence crisper.

An example of good plain words

Writing is harder when you lack the freedom to tackle interesting topics like music, marine life and football. Your writing day could be occupied by matters so humdrum they would make a great novelist weep: the rent for a piece of waste land; inefficient plumbing in the office toilets; a small rise in the price of custard.

Faced with a dull topic, there is great skill in creating a clear document that rises above the bland and boring. The following letter from an official to an anxious elderly couple is a model of simplicity. It doesn't give them everything they want – that would be an easy letter to write – but it does explain things reassuringly and fully. No doubt it could still be improved, but here it is, untouched:

Dear Mr and Mrs France

I write concerning an enquiry on your behalf by Councillor Jameson on several matters relating to your home. One of my colleagues will be writing to you about the bath, as I understand you are now having some difficulty with this.

As to the decoration of a further bedroom, I am arranging for the foreman painter to call and measure up in order to do the work.

I would expect this to be early in the new year so that the work can be done before the end of March.

At present there are no plans to install central heating in Jasmine Row. None of the properties in Jasmine Row were included in this year's programme. The programme of installations for next year and future years has not yet been drawn up and I cannot say at this stage whether Jasmine Row will be included in it.

It is our policy to install central heating in all our properties in the next few years, and we are steadily working towards this goal. As soon as I have any definite information I will write to you setting out our proposals.

If I can help further, please contact me.

Adjusting the style to the audience

Prominently placed in a hospital leaflet about healthy eating is a sentence taken from a UK Department of Health report, *Weaning and the Weaning Diet* (1994):

The provision of adequate dietary energy to ensure normal growth and development should be a principal determinant of the diets of children under five years of age.

This might be well understood by an audience of health professionals, but what if they wanted to get the same ideas across to a mass audience? Terms like 'principal determinant' and 'dietary energy' might be puzzling. According to the Department of Health, the latter just means 'calories', a technical term that is probably well understood by lay people who know it from diet guides. So the sentence holds an important message for parents of under 5's, namely, 'Give them plenty of calories, not muesli and skimmed milk, otherwise they could die of malnutrition' – which has indeed happened. One reason the sentence doesn't get this point across is that the verbs are feeble – 'should be' and the infinitive 'to ensure'. New life can be introduced through better verbs. For example, you could say:

To ensure that children under 5 grow and develop normally, one of the main things they need is calorie-rich food.

You would then continue by saying what else was needed, as you would if you were trying to get these points across to an individual parent:

While Helen is under 5, she needs food that has plenty of calories. This means things like a, b and c. These foods will help her to grow and develop normally. She also needs some x, y and z for taste and variety.

So while the original was in good English, it needed rewriting in plain English to meet the needs of a different audience. By doing so, an apparently complex idea can be communicated clearly in a way that will not short-change any of the audiences. This is not 'dumbing down' but clearing up.

What are regarded as common words may sometimes be misunderstood. A survey of 700 patients in an inner-city accident and emergency department found that half thought 'unconscious' people would still be able to hear; 41 per cent believed their eyes could not remain open after losing consciousness; 15 per cent thought they could still talk; and 15 per cent thought they could remain standing. The study, reported in the *Journal of Accident and Emergency Medicine*, has implications for anyone designing public health information including the scripts that emergency services use when responding to phone calls. In a leaflet, the signs of unconsciousness would have to be stated; in a call script, questions designed to test for unconsciousness would have to be included.

At Liverpool's Alder Hey hospital during the 1980s and 1990s, parents signed consent forms saying 'I hereby consent to a post mortem examination and to the removal of tissue (other than for the purpose of transplantation) at the time of this examination...'. They were unaware that this allowed doctors to harvest and store body parts and whole organ systems. Using similar consents, various hospitals are thought to have stored 150,000 organs. The word 'tissue', taken direct from the Human Tissue Act, wasn't apparently difficult. But its legal meaning differed from its everyday meaning and should have been explained. The misery resulting from this led to a government inquiry and fierce legal disputes.

The need to consider the audience is even more obvious in cross-cultural messages. This spam e-mail from the US blithely uses the phrase 'pledging a sorority', which is just as strange to British ears as 'plighting my troth' now seems to students of Middle English:

Hey there! My name is Michelle and I'm currently a freshman in
college. I've been a little busy lately cause I'm pledging a sorority but
I still find time to do stuff online.

Conquering fear

The main cause of bloated, show-off writing is fear. First there is fear
that being clear means being definite and that being definite leaves
no room for wriggling. Yet if writers want to hedge, a plain-English
style lets them. They can evoke a full range of doubt and uncertainty
– and even the possibility of being just plain wrong – with such words
as 'may', 'might', 'could', 'should', 'perhaps', 'normally' and 'generally'. Plain English doesn't always mean being unsubtle.

Then there is the fear that if you write simply you will not be
thought sufficiently eminent, scientific or literary. This fear was
examined in a research study in 1978. Over 1,500 scientists from
industry and the academic world were asked their opinion of two
short pieces of scientific writing. Both pieces gave exactly the same
facts in the same sequence of points, and used the same five technical terms. The only difference was in the style of the non-technical
language. The first version used everyday words and short, simply
constructed sentences. The second did the opposite, though without going to extremes. Nearly 70 per cent of the scientists preferred
the plain version; they also found it 'more stimulating' and 'more
interesting'. Three-quarters judged the writer to be more competent as a scientist and to have a better-organized mind.

So don't be afraid of plain English. Carefully used, it will reveal
your competence far better than the wooden style of so many academic and technical journals.

Plain English lexicon

If you overuse the words in the left-hand column of the table, your
writing could be perceived as pompous, officious and long-winded.
Not that anyone should forbid you from ever using them, but judi-
cious use of the alternatives will help you to be shorter, simpler and
more conversational. The alternatives are not always synonyms, so
use them with a proper care for meaning and for the job they have
to do in the sentence. In some contexts, words like 'remuneration',

'domicile' and 'residence' have technical meanings and cannot be substituted by their plainer alternatives.

Official-sounding terms	Plainer alternatives
accede	agree, grant, allow
accordingly	so
accustomed to	used to
acquaint yourself	find out, read
additional	more, extra
address (sense 'consider')	tackle, deal with, consider
advices	information, instructions
advise (sense 'inform')	inform, tell, let [me] know
aforementioned, aforesaid	[omit or be specific]
aggregate (noun)	total
alleviate	ease, reduce, lessen
apprise	inform, tell, let [me] know
as a consequence of	because
ascertain	find out
assist, assistance	help
attain	reach
attribute (verb)	earmark
category	group
cease	stop, end
cognizant of	aware of, know about
commence	start, begin
commensurate with	consistent with
component	part
concept	idea
concerning	about
consequently	so
constitute	make up, form
construe	interpret
corroboration	evidence, proof, support
deduct	take away, take off, subtract
deem	treat as, consider
defer	put off, postpone
desist	stop
despatch	send

Official-sounding terms	*Plainer alternatives*
despite the fact that	although, despite
determine	decide
determine (legal sense)	end, terminate
disburse	pay
discharge (verb)	pay off, settle
disconnect	cut off
discontinue	stop, end
due to the fact that	as, because
dwelling, domicile	home, property
elect, election	choose, choice
emanate from	come from, stem from
endeavour	try, attempt
entitlement	right
envisage	expect, imagine, forecast, think
equitable	fair
erroneous	wrong, mistaken
establish	set up, create, form
eventuate	result, occur, happen
expedite	hasten, speed up
expenditure	spending
expiration	end
facilitate	help
failure to	if you do not
for the duration of	during, while
for the purpose of	to
forward (verb)	send, give
furnish	give, provide
henceforth	from now on
heretofore	until now
herewith	with this
hitherto	until now
hypothecate	earmark
if this is not the case	if not
if this is the case	if so
impart	give, pass on, tell, inform
implement (verb)	carry out, do
in accordance with	in line with

Official-sounding terms	Plainer alternatives
inasmuch as	because, in that
incidence	rate of occurrence, how often
in conjunction with	with
increment	step, increase
indebtedness	debt
initiate	begin, start
in lieu of	instead of
in order to	to
in receipt of	get, have, receive, receiving
in regard to	about, concerning, on
insofar as	as far as
institute (verb)	begin, start
interim (noun)	meantime, for the time being
in the event of	if, when
in the eventuality of	if, when
in view of the fact that	as, because
manner	way
monies	money, amounts of money
necessitate	need, have to, require
nevertheless	even so, however, yet
nonetheless	even so, however, yet
not less than [ten]	at least [ten]
not more than [ten]	[ten] or less, [ten] or fewer
notwithstanding	even if, despite, still, yet, but
obtain	get, receive
other than	except
particulars	details, facts
persons	people
peruse	read or study carefully; examine
polemical	controversial
principal (adjective)	main, chief
prioritize	rank
prior to	before
provenance	source, origin
provisions [of a law, policy]	the law, the policy
purchase	buy
purport (verb)	pretend, claim, profess

Official-sounding terms	Plainer alternatives
pursuant to	under
reduction	cut
regarding	about
reimburse	repay
remittance	payment
remuneration	pay, wages, salary
remunerative employment	paid work
render	send, make, give
representations	comments
reside	live
residence	home, property, address
save (co-ordinator)	except
shall [legal obligation]	must
stipulate	state, set, lay down
sufficient	enough
supplementary	extra, more
terminate	end, stop
the law provides that	the law says
thereafter	then, afterwards
timeously	in good time
tranche	slice, portion, share, chunk
utilize	use
verify	check, prove
whensoever	when, whenever
whereby	by which, because of which
whilst	while
wilfully	deliberately
with reference to	about, concerning
with regard to	about, concerning
with respect to	about, for, concerning

Frequency count

It makes sense to use plain words in essential information because people are already familiar with them from other texts, as shown by their frequency in a set of 200 million words of contemporary British and American English collected by Oxford University Press. The figures below show frequency per million words.

Official-sounding terms	*Plainer alternatives*
accordingly *23*	so *2021*
advices *0.1*	information *496*, instructions *38*
attain *18*	reach *236*
category *81*	group *514*
cease *25*	stop *220*
commence *13*	begin *454*
concept *115*	idea *324*
entitlement *6.51*	right *388*
forward (verb) *6.55*	send *226*
initiate *24*	begin *454*
in the event of *8.12*	if *2461*
monies *2.89*	money *320*
notwithstanding *7.53*	despite *150*
particulars *4.29*	details *107*
persons *43*	people *1175*
prior to *26*	before *860*
purchase *62*	buy *235*
regarding *44*	about *1943*
shall *162*	must *667*
terminate *12*	end *151*
utilise/utilize *24*	use *1424*
whilst *45*	while *667*

The figures do not fully compare like with like because it was not possible to examine the senses in which the words were used. However, the frequency counts reflect the plurals of all the nouns listed, and all forms of the verbs.

The *Collins Cobuild English Dictionary* is a useful source on word frequency. It also gives information about the grammatical framework that particular words tend to inhabit, and with which other words they usually combine. This can be helpful in creating sentence structures that readers will be familiar with.

A word on some troublesome words

address 'We are addressing the problem and will let you have a reply soon.' Occasionally ambiguity arises from the use of 'address' in this way: 'The minister has been addressing the letter he received from Mr Smith.' Cynics also say the verb is often used as a cover for inaction. More precise verbs are usually available, such as 'consider' and 'tackle'.

advices Still a favourite pomposity among lawyers: 'I await your advices in respect of this matter.' Better to be precise and use 'instructions', 'suggestions' or 'comments'.

advise Near-universal business English for 'inform', 'tell' or 'let me know', but to avoid ambiguity it is better to use one of these and keep 'advise' for 'give advice to'. This avoids such officialese as 'please be advised that your cheque is in the post' which, apart from usually being untrue, begins with four redundant words.

and/or The oblique puts the reader to the trouble of creating three possible meanings. Instead of writing 'We will bring horses and/or donkeys', prefer 'We will bring horses or donkeys or both.' When used in legal documents, and/or has caused much litigation. If you can avoid it, do so.

anticipate Often used as a posh word for 'expect'. Their different meanings should not be allowed to merge, say careful users. 'Anticipate' means to take some action to forestall, or benefit from, a future event:

Customers anticipated the rise in interest rates by choosing fixed-rate loans.

apropos or **à propos** Prefer 'about', 'concerning' or 'with reference to'.

as and when This never seems to mean anything more than 'when' or 'if':

As and when the go-ahead is given, the project will involve the construction of a new underground station as well as rail tunnels

– which probably means:

As soon as we get the go-ahead for the project, we will begin constructing a new underground station and rail tunnels.

as at 'The value of your shares as at 5 April was £324.' Normally 'on' will do.

as per 'I enclose the form as per our conversation.' It's better, if not always possible, to avoid mixing English and Latin in the same phrase. Prefer 'I enclose the form as discussed.' Alternatively, 'in accordance with' will often do the job. 'As per usual' is especially cringe-making.

at the end of the day This is waffle for 'ultimately', 'eventually' or 'in the end'. The only thing that really occurs 'at the end of the day' is nightfall.

avail yourself 'If you fail to avail yourself of the facilities above, your electricity supply could be cut off without further notice.' Avoid such woolly, pseudo-genteel expressions. Prefer 'If you do not use [or 'take up' or 'make use of'] one of the repayment methods shown above . . .'.

brainchild This is journalese for 'idea'. If you have several ideas, please do not call them brainchildren.

can Careful users are very careful with 'can' and 'may'. The first means 'is able to' as in 'Helen can take solid food now that her jaw is mended.' The second means 'is permitted to', as in 'Helen may take solid food because the doctor says it's safe to do so.' The second meaning is common in legal documents:

The secretary of state may make rules requiring a patents register to be kept. The rules may delegate the keeping of the register to another person.

Concern that 'may' will not be understood correctly has led to at least one credit-card company trying to explain it in its terms and conditions:

If we agree with another person or business (the transferee) for it to take over all our rights and obligations under this agreement, we may (but do not have to) give you at least 30 days' notice beforehand.

This is odd because the rest of the document uses 'may' freely without a similar explanation (eg, 'We may introduce and vary charges in the future.') A court might well decide that the two forms of 'may' were meant to have different meanings.

'May' can also imply a positive possibility:

You should show this letter to other joint shareholders as they may receive different information from elsewhere

whereas 'might' in that position would suggest that the possibility was more remote. In practice most people use 'may' and 'might' interchangeably in such situations, to the fury of pedants.

disconnect 'We regret that your supply could be disconnected unless you make a satisfactory arrangement to pay the arrears.' It used to be impossible to persuade electricity and gas suppliers to use the plainer 'cut off' – it was thought to be 'not quite nice'. Now they all do it.

documentation 'We will let you have the documentation in the next ten days.' This is pompous: 'documents' will do.

duly If this means anything, it means 'in the correct manner'. A company's share-offer letter includes a rash of dulys:

I am pleased to tell you that . . . as a qualifying shareholder, an application for shares duly made by you . . . will receive special treatment . . . This means that, if you duly apply in the offer . . . If you duly apply on this application form . . .

The company could have avoided the word by saying on the application form that only correctly completed forms would qualify for the offer.

etc (Latin: et cetera, meaning 'the rest'.) This is perhaps the best understood Latin abbreviation and, though sometimes labelled '*e*xtreme *t*hought *c*ollapse', is harmless if used in moderation and if precision is not required:

The burglar stole televisions, videos etc.

If a list is introduced by a word like 'such as' or 'includes', 'etc' is unnecessary because the reader knows the list is incomplete:

The stolen goods included televisions, videos and stereos.

general consensus of opinion 'Consensus' covers it, in a word. And it needs three *s*'s.

get, got Primary-school teachers' exasperation at the overuse of these words has left many people afraid to use them at all in formal writing. The alternatives 'receive' and 'obtain' are plain enough but there's no harm in 'get' and 'got' (words with a thousand years of common use behind them) when you feel that their simplicity and informality are helpful:

I got your letter yesterday. Thank you for keeping me informed. I'll send someone around to fix the problem.

If your managers dislike the words, quote Proverbs at them:

Wisdom is the principal thing therefore get wisdom and with all thy getting get understanding

which doubles as a counterblast to people who say you shouldn't repeat the same word in a sentence or paragraph.

having said that or **that having been said** A waffling way of writing 'but', 'however' or 'even so'. Addicts can withdraw slowly with 'that said'.

hence A useful but regrettably uncommon word. It can mean 'as a result' ('hence the election will take place next week') or 'from now' ('The election will take place two weeks hence'). Use the word regularly or it will disappear.

herewith, hereby, hereof, heretofore, hereinbefore, hereto, herein These smell of old law books; they are not plain words. 'I hereby declare' just means 'I declare'. 'The document attached hereto' just means 'the document attached' or 'the document attached to this'. Happily, these words are slowly disappearing from business and legal use. Such linguistic change often occurs and should cause no-one to fear the imminent death of the language. Do we miss, for example, a range of once-common words beginning with the 'wan-' prefix: 'wanthrift' (extravagance), 'wanhap' (misfortune), 'wantruth' (falsehood) and 'wanchance' (ill-luck)? Only 'wanton' (undisciplined) remains in fairly common use.

however As this is often used as a more leisurely alternative to 'but', it is usually preceded and followed by a comma:

It seems clear that your opponent lied in court. We do not believe, however, that she is likely to be convicted of perjury.

If 'however' begins a sentence – often the best position, since it tells the reader immediately what sort of point is coming up – a comma will normally follow:

However, we do not believe that she is likely to be convicted of perjury.

The next sentence shows a common mistake with 'however':

You have told us that the ring was stolen while the back door was left open, however, the policy only covers theft from your home if force is used to enter or leave.

Because 'however' seems to lengthen the pause that precedes it, effectively creating a second sentence, a comma is not enough. A semicolon or full stop (see also chapter 11) would be better:

You have told us that the ring was stolen while the back door was left open. However, the policy only covers theft from your home if force is used to enter or leave.

Or you could use 'but' and save some of the punctuation:

You have told us that the ring was stolen while the back door was left open, but the policy only covers theft from your home if force was used to enter or leave.

Obviously there is no need for a comma after 'however' in such phrases as 'However likeable he was, he had a vicious streak.'

impact on/with 'The defeat will impact on us badly.' Use 'affect' – 'The defeat will affect us badly.' It saves a word and shows you can tell your affects from your effects.

I write or **I am writing** Many writers are told not to begin letters with these phrases because it's obvious they are writing. But 'I write to explain the department's policy on . . .' is quite harmless – you could not launch in with 'I explain . . .'. On the other hand 'I write to inform you that' might as well be deleted, as nothing useful has been said.

meet up with In British English, 'meet' alone will do.

methodology This means a body of methods or the study of method and its application in a particular field. It is often mis-used as a posh word for 'method'.

Ms This, pronounced 'miz', is now the courtesy title of choice for many women who do not wish their marital status to be disclosed by 'Miss' or 'Mrs'. Use it unless the woman has asked to be addressed by a different title. If a woman signs her letters 'Susan Hopkins' without indicating a preferred title, there is no harm in writing to her as 'Dear Susan Hopkins' or 'Dear Ms Hopkins'.

null and void 'Null' means 'void' ('of no effect'), so there's no need for both words in a phrase like 'The agreement is null and void'. Simplest is 'void' or 'worthless'.

opine 'The barrister opined that the case would fail in court.' This unusual verb smells of pomposity in British English and is best avoided. This is a pity as it leads to wordiness like 'It is the opinion of the barrister that . . .'. Alternative verbs include 'believe', 'consider', 'say'.

prior to This pompous way of saying 'before' has escaped from its cage and bred plentifully. It tends to produce clumsy, verbless constructions: 'Prior to the abandonment of the mine by the company . . .' instead of 'Before the company abandoned the mine . . .'. It is better to keep 'prior' as an adjective – 'prior approval', 'prior discussion' – or as a noun for people in charge of monasteries.

re 'Re: Claim for housing benefit.' A Latin remnant from the word 'res' ('a thing'), this is not a short form of 'reference' or 'regarding'. The word should be struck out of all headings to letters and e-mails – let them stand on their own. In text, prefer 'about', 'concerning' or 'on'. When referring to cases, lawyers often use 're' to mean 'in the matter of': 'Re [or even *In re*] Casaubon 1992'. Better is 'In Casaubon 1992'.

shall The old rule was that when writing of future events you would say 'I *shall*; you will; he/she/it will; we *shall*; you (plural) will; they will' but that when writing of promises, obligations or commands, the *wills* and *shalls* would change places. This is why the British coronation oath goes:

Archbishop: Will you to your power cause law and justice, with mercy, to be executed in all your judgments?

Sovereign: I will.

And it's why Binyon's poem of 1914, often quoted in memory of the war dead, says:

They shall grow not old, as we that are left grow old,
Age shall not weary them, nor the years condemn.
At the going down of the sun and in the morning
We will remember them.

But only one person in a million now understands these distinctions, so there is confusion when legal documents use 'shall' in an effort to impose an obligation. 'Must' is clearer for this purpose: 'The tenant must pay the rent on time.' Conveniently for people who take this view, the Old English root of 'shall' is 'sceal', meaning 'I must' or 'I owe'. The Oxford University Press figures referred to earlier in this chapter show 162 uses of 'shall', so it is still common, but 667 of 'must'. For legal prohibitions, 'may not' and 'must not' are widely used, though the latter has been condemned as barbarous by at least one judge.

should Traditionally this was the correct form of the conditional tense in the first person singular and plural. Or, in plain English, it was right to say 'I *should*; you would; he/she/it would; we *should*; you would; they would.' This is why many still prefer to write: 'I should be grateful if you would . . .' not 'I would be grateful if you could ...' or 'I would be grateful if you would ...'. A neat sidestep is to write 'I'd be grateful if you would ...' or 'Would you please ...'.

to hand 'I have to hand your letter of 15 January.' This is the kind of snooty language that gets bureaucrats a bad name. Avoid it with 'thank you' or 'I refer to'.

unless and until 'Unless and until the conditions are met, the deal is off.' This usage smells of officialdom. Either 'unless' or 'until' will do.

whilst This is becoming unusual (especially in American English). Its job has been usurped by 'while', with which it is interchangeable as a co-ordinator in standard English.

Words often confused

Your documents will seem unprofessional if you muddle up similar-sounding words, like these:

- *affect* (verb) means to alter or change ('Damage to the rudder affected the steering.') or pretend ('They affected not to listen.').
- *effect* (verb) means to do, make, implement, bring about, accomplish.

- *affect* (noun) means an emotion, feeling or desire.
- *effect* (noun) means a result.

- *criteria* is the plural of criterion.

- *desserts* are puddings, only.
- *deserts* are what you deserve (eg, 'just deserts'), or wastelands.

- *defused* means that a fuse has been taken out or, figuratively, that tension has been lessened ('The row was defused by immediate action.').
- *diffused* means to spread widely ('Light diffused throughout the cellar.').

- *discreet* means tactful, secretive, trustworthy, circumspect.
- *discrete* means separate, individually distinct.

- *flaunt* means to act in a showy or brazen way.
- *flout* means to disobey or show contempt for.

- *hone* means to polish, refine, sharpen ('They honed their blades and waited.').
- *home* means to move in on or focus ('He homed in on this bright idea.').

- *imply* means to suggest or indicate ('She implied she had never married.').
- *infer* means deduce, draw an inference from ('The pathologist inferred she had had several children.').

- *incidence* means rate of occurrence, and is singular ('The incidence of HIV/AIDS is rising in the Baltic states.')
- *incident* is an event.
- *instance* is an occasion or occurrence ('There have been several recent instances of needle-stick injuries.').

- *mitigate* means to excuse or lessen the severity ('His guilty plea mitigated the sentence.').
- *militate* against means to operate powerfully against.

- *moot* means to put forward or float an idea.

- *mute* means silent or to silence.
- *phenomena* is the plural of phenomenon.
- *principle* is a rule of conduct ('He lived according to his principles.').
- *principal* means main, chief ('Our principal aim is world domination.'), or a sum of money on which interest is payable.
- *refute* and *rebut* mean to disprove by argument or evidence.
- *deny*, *reject* and *repudiate* mean to dispute a statement without using argument or evidence.

Foreign words

English is certainly the richer for its contact with foreign words, with hundreds of direct borrowings like 'caravan', 'trek', 'graffiti', 'bastard', 'clan', 'crag', 'criterion', 'phenomenon', 'slogan', 'corgi', 'garage' and 'armada'. Then there are thousands of foreign-derived words such as 'plant', 'fantasy', 'custom', 'interest', 'jury', 'mutton' and 'tea'. (For an account of the history of such words, see any large single-volume dictionary.)

It's not always easy to judge which foreign words have gained enough currency to be well understood. 'Ad hoc', in such phrases as 'ad hoc group' and 'ad hoc committee', usefully fills a gap. The terms 'ie' and 'eg' will be understood by a professional audience and benefit from being concise, but for a mass audience the English equivalents are safer. Times have certainly changed. In 1939 a famous book on punctuation began:

> In writing this book I have had more especially in mind three classes of readers: those who, professionally or otherwise, are faced with the task of reading proofs; those who at school are learning to write English correctly (and perhaps a few of their teachers, *quorum pars parva fui*); and those ordinary folk – I have met plenty – who remark somewhat vaguely 'I know nothing about punctuation' . . .

Most authors today would feel obliged to give a translation of the Latin phrase (it means 'of which I was once one'). Around the turn of the new century, the BBC dropped its award-winning science series 'QED' because few viewers knew what the title meant or that it had any connection with science. The series has been reinvented as 'Living Proof'. Using uncommon foreign-language terms may look like showing off, so unless you are sure of your audience avoid those words so often seen in the literary review pages like 'oeuvre', 'Bildungsroman' and 'auteur'. If you want your staff to provide a guide or a briefing note, don't ask them for a 'vade mecum'. Writing in the Johns Hopkins Magazine in 1991, the academics R Wallers and T H Kern tell students: 'Avoid using the Latin terms *ibid.*, *op cit.*, and *loc cit.* Odds are, you don't know what they really mean, and neither do most professors.'

Some terms haven't entirely lost their strangeness but have made the transition into plain English. In this group are 'vice versa', which saves the writer many words of explanation (though 'the other way round' or 'on the contrary' are sometimes good enough), 'per cent' and 'etc'. 'Curriculum vitae' seems likely to endure, shortened to 'CV'. The best alternative that American English can come up with is French – résumé – while in south-east Asia the pleasing 'biodata' is widespread.

Latin still fights a rearguard action on the British pound coin, where it is more heavily represented than English or Welsh with phrases like 'Nemo me impune lacessit' ('No-one harms me and gets away with it') and 'Decus et tutamen' ('Glory and protection'). Latin's conciseness undoubtedly helps when space is tight, but its use on the currency suggests that the plain languages of the UK are not thought good enough for some ceremonial purposes. Tendring District Council's official crest hedges its bets by offering the Latin and English together: 'Pro bono omnium' and 'For the good of all'.

Latin or French [F] phrase	Meaning or alternative phrase
ad hoc	for this purpose or occasion
carte blanche [F]	a free hand, freedom
ceteris paribus	other things being equal
cf (conferre)	compare
circa	about
de minimis	trivialities, small amounts
eg (exempli gratia)	such as, for example
en bloc [F]	as a whole, together

Latin or French [F] phrase	Meaning or alternative phrase
etc (et cetera)	and so on, and the rest
ex officio	by virtue of the office held
ibid (ibidem)	in same place, book etc; same source
ie (id est)	that is
inter alia/alios	among other things/people
loc cit	passage cited above
modus operandi	way of working, method
mutatis mutandis	with the necessary changes
op cit (opus citatum)	work quoted
per annum	per year, a year, annually
per capita	per head, per person, each
per diem	per day, a day, daily
per se	as such, by or in itself, essentially
pp (per procurationem)	on behalf of, by the agency of
pro forma	a form
QED	proved as required
qv (quod vide)	see
seriatim	one at a time; in the same order
sic	thus! (drawing notice to an error)
sine die	indefinitely
vis-à-vis [F]	as regards, regarding, on, about
viz (videlicet)	namely
vs (versus)	v, versus, against
vs (vide supra)	see above

3 | Writing tight

Guideline: *Use only as many words as you really need.*

Flab. Writing is full of it. These 95 words from a loan company tell borrowers they have fallen behind with their repayments. More than a third can be cut without losing any meaning:

> Arrears at present subsist on your mortgage account in the sum of £1,032, with a further payment becoming due on the 11th April. In view of the account being a mortgage account, we are not in a position to stop interest being debited each month and in order to prevent the account situation from deteriorating, it is necessary that payments are received each month which represent the interest debit. At present this amount is £242 and therefore it is regretted your offer to make payments in the sum of £80 a month is not sufficient.

You may like to blue-pencil it yourself, but at the end of the chapter we'll see how so many words can be saved.

Part of writing well is writing tight, ruthlessly cutting dross. Most readers are busy people who want the main points of your message, and fast. Making them read excess words is an unfriendly act, especially in business where a deluge of unwanted paper and e-mails falls on everyone at every level. Not that shorter is always better: sometimes you need more words to make a point clear. Plain, certainly. Tight, certainly. But not so plain or tight that you miss out essential points or seem blunt and rude. Being ruthless with words needn't mean being graceless with people.

Cutting dross enables your information to shine more clearly. In the early 1900s, Professor William Strunk used to tell his students: 'Omit needless words, omit needless words, omit needless words.' (Once should have been enough, but he was keen.) He believed that just as drawings should have no unnecessary lines and machines no unnecessary parts, so sentences should have no unnecessary words.

Easy to agree with, perhaps, but hard to do. The key is to let the first draft stand as long as possible, then return and revise it. Then revise it again. And probably again. In business, of course, time is against you: that letter or report must go out tonight. And useless words aren't always obvious – they have to be hunted. So let's examine the three main techniques for dealing with them:

1   Striking out useless words.

2   Pruning the dead wood, grafting on the vigorous.

3   Rewriting completely.

Striking out useless words

The most obviously useless words are straight repetition:

The cheque that was received from Classic Assurance was received on 13 January.

'Was received' occurs twice, so the sentence could say:

The cheque ~~that was received~~ from Classic Assurance was received on 13 January

or

The cheque ~~that was received~~ from Classic Assurance ~~was received~~ arrived on 13 January.

Spotting this kind of thing becomes harder as the distance between repetitions increases:

The standard of traffic management on the A57, A59 and A623 is of a lower standard than on other major roads in the region.

It doesn't make sense to say that a 'standard . . . is of a lower standard', so the rewrite would be:

The standard of traffic management on the A57, A59 and A623 is ~~of a~~ lower ~~standard~~ than on other major roads in the region.

Then there are words that repeat an idea:

We attach herewith a financial statement.

If the statement is attached – or enclosed – it must be 'herewith', so the word can disappear.

Journalists occasionally succumb, too. 'In a strongly worded blistering attack at the HFEA's conference, Ms Leather will accuse Prof Zanos of "breathtaking hubris".' If the attack is to be blistering, it will doubtless be strongly worded, so those words can be omitted.

Wordiness often comes from trying to make a simple procedure sound impressive:

A new bank account is in the process of being set up for you.

Delete four words and this becomes:

A new bank account is ~~in the process of~~ being set up for you.

The verb 'carry out' (like 'undertake' and 'perform') always merits suspicion; often a more vigorous expression will make the same point more economically. For example, it can simply be deleted:

Work is required to be carried out on the flue and funnels

becomes:

Work is required ~~to be carried out~~ on the flue and funnels.

Or 'carry out' can be cut by strengthening the verb it supports:

The firm does not intend to remove the lime trees but it is necessary to carry out pruning to the trees to keep them healthy.

This becomes:

The firm does not intend to remove the lime trees but it is necessary to ~~carry out pruning to~~ prune the trees to keep them healthy

or

The firm does not intend to remove the lime trees and pruning will keep them healthy.

It's not always so easy to see redundancy. Take this sentence:

For the benefit of new members, the secretary described the rules of the committee and the remit that had been given to it.

Since 'remit' means the committee's terms of reference and a remit must, by its nature, be 'given', the last six words are redundant:

For the benefit of new members, the secretary described the rules of the committee and ~~the~~ its remit ~~that had been given to it~~.

You can safely cut out useless phrases like 'it should be pointed out that', 'it must be noted that', 'I should mention that', 'I would inform you that' and 'I would stress that'. Better just to point it out, note it, mention it, or stress it. In the following examples, the useless words are underlined; what remains makes perfectly good sense on its own:

<u>I must point out that</u> I am legally obliged to charge rates on the property's current value.

I <u>would like to take this opportunity to</u> apologize for the delay in replying to your complaint.

<u>It should be appreciated that</u> there is always an element of under-reporting of accidents, particularly if no-one is injured. <u>It should</u> also <u>be noted that</u> our accident figures exclude occurrences where the system for explosion relief operated effectively.

<u>It is only fair for me to point out at this point that</u> the committee showed great concern about your case at its last meeting.

<u>This letter is to advise you that</u>, following our successful seminar last year for suppliers, we plan to hold another on 13 October.

Pruning the dead wood, grafting on the vigorous

Dead wood often makes a fine pretence of being alive, so a keen eye is needed. In this example, 10 unnecessary words could be replaced by one:

May I draw your attention to the final account dated 28 June from which I note that six payments of £18 were credited to your account from 28 March to 25 August, totalling £108.

The first six words are courteous but they delay the main message unduly and could go. Then, 'from which I note' is pompous – what matters is not what the writer notes but what the final account shows. Using the vigorous verb 'shows', the sentence becomes:

~~May I draw your attention to~~ the final account dated 28 June ~~from which I note~~ shows that six payments of £18 were credited to your account from 28 March to 25 August, totalling £108.

Certain words are prime suspects for pruning. They include 'situation', 'aspect', 'facility', 'issue', 'element', 'factor', 'matter' and 'concept'. All are occasionally useful but they tend to be overworked at the expense of more concrete words:

The company has one engineer on call at all times, giving excellent speed of response in emergency situations.

An 'emergency situation' is nothing more than an emergency, so 'situation' can safely be cut:

The company has one engineer on call at all times, giving excellent speed of response in emergencies.

Another phrase often accompanied by verbiage is 'the fact'. There is 'given the fact that' and 'in the light of the fact that' (which just mean 'as' or 'since'); 'despite the fact that' (which means 'although'); and 'the fact of the matter is' (which, if it means anything, means 'the fact is'). Here, the six deleted words could simply be replaced by 'As':

> ~~In view of the fact that~~ the central heating was fitted by Union Gas, they have cancelled the bill in the interests of good customer relations.

Rewriting completely

When there are far too many words for the message but neither of the first two methods will work, a total rewrite is the only alternative. Various signals may alert you to this need:

- The meaning isn't clear.
- The sentence is long and the verbs are few.
- The verbs are feeble – for example, they are smothered by nouns (see chapter 5), they are in the passive voice (see chapter 4), or they are derived from 'to be' or 'to have' (see chapter 4).

For example, an engineer is writing about the cost of materials for a road scheme:

> Over-estimating on one type of material could have a detrimental cost effect for the clients, depending on the prices in the Bill of Quantities.

Alarm bells ring at 'have a detrimental cost effect'. First because 'have' seems feeble as the solitary verb in the sentence, and second because 'detrimental cost effect' is a pompous way of expressing the simple idea that the clients might have to pay more. So the whole sentence could say:

> Over-estimating on one type of material could cost the clients more, depending on the prices in the Bill of Quantities.

While this saves only four words, there is now a strong verb, 'cost', and the message is immediately apparent.

An insurance firm is thinking of publishing a guidance booklet for managers of company car fleets. Its internal report on the idea begins:

AIM OF PROPOSED CAR FLEET MANAGEMENT GUIDE

This guide would have the objective of highlighting to car fleet managers the best way to achieve, and the benefits of adopting, a professional approach vis-à-vis managing a car fleet.

There are only a few publications at present covering the subject of car fleet management and with no current insurance company involvement there would appear to be a definite market niche for us to explore.

This makes sense but is far too flabby:

- 'Would have the objective of highlighting' is a wordy way of saying 'aims' or 'seeks'.
- In plain words, 'vis-à-vis' means 'towards' or 'to'.
- Sentences beginning 'there are', 'there is' and 'there were' are often wordy and reduce the strength of any remaining verbs. Two 'there' verbs are present here.
- In 'the subject of car fleet management', the first three words are redundant because readers know from the heading that 'car fleet management' is a subject.
- 'No current insurance company involvement' smothers the verb 'involve' (see chapter 5). In any case, a more expressive verb would be 'publish' or 'produce'.
- 'Insurance company' could be cut to 'insurer'.

So a first redraft might say:

AIM OF PROPOSED CAR FLEET MANAGEMENT GUIDE

This guide would show car fleet managers how they could best achieve a professional approach to managing a car fleet and the benefits of doing so.

At present, only a few publications cover car fleet management. None of them is produced by insurers so there is a definite market niche for us to explore.

A second redraft would go a little further:

AIM OF PROPOSED CAR FLEET MANAGEMENT GUIDE

This guide would show car fleet managers how to do their work more professionally and why this would benefit them.

Few publications cover car fleet management, none of them produced by insurers. So there is a definite market niche for us to explore.

The original had 72 words, this has 52. What remains is tight and doesn't waste the reader's time.

Putting it all together

The chapter began by promising to cut more than a third from a letter to a mortgage payer. First, useless words can go:

> Arrears ~~at present~~ subsist on your mortgage account ~~in the sum~~ of £1,032, with a further payment ~~becoming~~ due on ~~the~~ 11~~th~~ April. ~~In view of the account being a mortgage account~~, we are not in a position to stop interest being debited ~~each month~~ and ~~in order~~ to prevent the account ~~situation~~ from deteriorating, it is necessary that payments are received each month which represent the interest debit. At present this amount is £242 ~~and~~ therefore it is regretted that your offer to ~~make~~ pay~~ments in the sum of~~ £80 a month is not sufficient.

Then vigorous words (underlined) can be grafted on:

> <u>The</u> arrears ~~subsist~~ on your mortgage account ~~of~~ <u>are</u> £1,032, <u>and</u> ~~with~~ a further payment <u>is</u> due on 11 April. Regrettably we ~~are not in a position to~~ <u>cannot</u> stop interest being ~~debited~~ <u>charged</u>. Therefore, to prevent the ~~account from deteriorating,~~ <u>arrears growing</u>, ~~it is necessary that~~ <u>you will need to pay the interest charge</u> ~~are received~~ each month ~~which represent the interest debit~~. At present this ~~amount~~ is £242, ~~therefore~~ <u>so</u> ~~it is regretted~~ <u>we regret</u> that your offer to pay £80 a month is not sufficient.

So the final version is:

> The arrears on your mortgage account are £1,032, and a further payment is due on 11 April. Regrettably we cannot stop interest being charged. Therefore, to prevent the arrears growing, you will need to pay the interest charge each month. At present this is £242, so we regret that your offer to pay £80 a month is not sufficient.

This is only 59 words, a cut of 37 per cent. It delivers the same facts and is just as courteous – perhaps more so.

Results from the focus group showed a strong preference for the final version over the original. The final version scored an average clarity mark of 17 points out of a possible 20, as against only 10 for the original. Twenty-nine people out of 34 preferred the final version.

4 | Favouring the active voice

Guideline: *Prefer the active voice unless there's a good reason for using the passive.*

This sentence has an active-voice verb:

Fred is demolishing the building

while this has a passive-voice verb:

The building is being demolished by Fred.

This chapter explains:

- the difference between active and passive;
- how to convert one to the other;
- why the active should be your first choice;
- how 'I' and 'we' can make formal reports more readable;
- when the passive can be useful.

During a series of plain-language workshops in India, I was surprised that so many of the lawyers and government officials who attended could readily distinguish between active- and passive-voice verbs. Most of them had learned English as a second language and had had to master the basics of its grammar. Yet in countries where English is the first language, 'active' and 'passive' are often alien terms that native English speakers meet only when they study a second language. This is a pity, as the ability to recognize and use the active voice helps to foster a plain-English style.

Many writers have damned the passive voice unreservedly. In 1946, George Orwell wrote: 'Never use the passive where you can use the active'. But this is going much too far. Certainly the active tends to make the writing tighter, more personal, and introduces action earlier in sentences. The passive tends to do the reverse. Yet the passive is still a valuable tool, as we will see.

The words 'passive' and 'active' are well understood in their everyday meanings: 'Some men take an active role in infant care, but many are passive.' These everyday meanings differ from their grammatical ones. So, as you read this chapter, please suppress the everyday meanings.

Recognizing active-voice verbs ('active verbs', for short)

Putting the 'doer' – the person or thing doing the action in the sentence – in front of its verb will usually ensure that the verb is active. The following sentences all have active verbs (underlined) because the doers precede the verbs they govern:

The President <u>wants</u> an improved health service.

I <u>walked</u> up the stairs.

Armies <u>are</u> on the march.

She <u>hates</u> going to work.

Ice-cream <u>tastes</u> revolting.

Most of us favour active verbs when we speak. People would think you odd if you continually said things like 'The house is being bought by me' (passive) instead of 'I am buying the house' (active), though the meaning is the same if they are spoken with the same stresses.

Occasionally a verb can be followed by a doer yet remain active:

She used to hate going to work, said her sister.

Here 'her sister' follows 'said' but the verb is still in the active because 'said her sister' is grammatically identical to 'her sister said'.

Recognizing passive-voice verbs ('passive verbs', for short)

In most sentences with a passive verb, the doer follows the verb or is not stated, as here (verbs underlined):

(a) Three mistakes <u>were admitted</u> by the director.

(b) Coastal towns <u>are being damaged</u> by storms.

(c) Verdicts <u>will</u> soon <u>be delivered</u> in the Smith case.

In (a) and (b), the doers ('director' and 'storms') follow the verbs through which they act. In (c) the doer is not stated; no-one can tell who or what will give the verdicts.

To put (a) and (b) into the active, you simply bring the doer to the start of the sentence:

The director admitted three mistakes.

Storms are damaging coastal towns.

To convert (c) into the active, you would need to know the doer:

[The judge] will soon deliver verdicts in the Smith case.

An almost infallible test for passives is to check whether the verb consists of:

- part of the verb 'to be' (though this is sometimes implied rather than stated, as in many newspaper headlines where space is tight – 'Explorer [is] attacked in jungle'); and
- a past participle.

This is an easy test to apply if you can already recognize parts of 'to be' and past participles. If not, here's how:

Parts of the verb 'to be'

Present tense (explained in chapter 13): am, is, are, am being, is being, are being.

Past tenses: was, were, has been, have been, had been.

Future tense: will be, shall be.

Infinitive (explained in chapter 13): to be.

Be careful, however, not to confuse parts of 'to be' with parts of 'to have', which are 'has', 'had' and 'have'. The difference is clear from the expressions 'You are a frog' and 'You have a frog'. The first is about being, the second possession.

Past participle

All verbs have a past participle. To find it, begin with the infinitive form of the verb, for example:

to attract   to annoy   to decide   to go

Cross out 'to' and send the rest into the past tense:

to attract + ed   to annoy + ed

to decide + d   to go + ne or went

The first three are past participles. In the fourth, you need to apply a tie-break by putting 'we have' in front of each phrase, producing 'we have gone' and 'we have went'. Only the first of these makes sense in standard English, so 'gone' is the past participle while 'went' is just a past tense. The tie-break is useful because some common verbs have two candidates for past participle: 'see' (seen/saw); 'eat' (eaten/ate); 'take' (taken/took); and 'give' (given/gave). Applying the tie-break reveals that the first alternative is the past participle in each case.

Applying the full test for passives to the example sentences, it is clear that they all fulfil its criteria:

(a) **Three mistakes <u>were admitted</u> by the director.**
(b) **Coastal towns <u>are being damaged</u> by storms.**
(c) **Verdicts <u>will</u> soon <u>be delivered</u> in the Smith case.**

In (c) the fact that 'soon' is splitting the verb makes no difference – the verb 'will be delivered' is still passive.

Computerized grammar checkers search for passives by applying the same test. Unfortunately this will occasionally throw up phantom passives. For example, 'is tired' would be flagged as a passive in the sentence:

A man who is tired of London is tired of life

as it appears to fulfil the criteria of having part of 'to be' and the past participle of 'to tire'. But it cannot be a passive because no doer can be attached to 'is tired' and none is implied. 'Tired' in each case is a description of the man, not part of the verb. The verb 'is' is in the active voice. The same logic applies to sentences like this:

The directors are concerned about the new runway

– where 'are' is active and 'concerned' is not a verb but a description of the directors' state of mind.

Converting passives to actives

Though using the active in the examples that follow will produce only small gains in clarity and economy, a general preference for active over passive will significantly improve the readability of most documents.

A financial adviser writes to his client:

We have been asked by your home insurers to obtain your written confirmation that all their requirements have been completed by yourself.

By applying the test, 'have been asked' and 'have been completed' are revealed as passives. Use of the active, putting the doers in front of the verbs, would give:

Your home insurers have asked us to obtain your written confirmation that you have completed all their requirements.

I wanted to see whether the focus group would record any preference between these two versions, as the only difference is in the use of active and passive. Though the groups regarded both as clear (13 points out of 20 for the passive sentence, 17 for the active), 28 people out of 35 preferred the active – a striking result.

A safety official writes (passives underlined):

A recommendation <u>was made</u> by inspectors that consideration <u>be given</u> by the company to the fitting of an interlock trip between the ventilation systems to prevent cell pressurisation.

Converting passive to active, the sentence becomes (actives underlined):

Inspectors <u>made</u> a recommendation that the company <u>give</u> consideration to the fitting of an interlock trip between the ventilation systems to prevent cell pressurisation.

Then, using the strong verbs hidden beneath 'recommendation' and 'consideration', the sentence becomes even crisper – and 10 words shorter than the original:

Inspectors <u>recommended</u> that the company <u>consider</u> fitting an interlock trip between the ventilation systems to prevent cell pressurisation.

In the focus group, 18 people out of 35 preferred this final version over the passive sentence. Nine preferred the passive, while the others couldn't decide.

Verbs provide so much useful information that readers prefer to get them early in sentences; this tends not to happen when the verbs are passive. Placing an important verb late forces readers to store large chunks of text in their short-term memory while they wait to discover the doer and what the action will be. The problem is worsened if there are other hurdles, like brackets containing exceptions and qualifications:

If you decide to cancel your application, a cheque for the amount of your investment (subject to a deduction of the amount (if any) by

**which the value of your investment has fallen at the date at which
your cancellation form is received by us) will be sent to you.**

'You decide' and 'has fallen' are active, while 'is received' and 'will
be sent' are passive. 'Will be sent' needs converting into the active
because it is too far (36 words) from the noun it refers to, which is
'cheque'. Making this single change would produce:

**If you decide to cancel your application, <u>we will send you</u> a cheque
for the amount of your investment (subject to a deduction of the
amount (if any) by which the value of your investment has fallen at
the date at which your cancellation form is received by us) ~~will be
sent to you~~.**

This would be the first stage in a comprehensive kill of brackets
and other debris that would produce:

**If you decide to cancel your application, we will send you a cheque
for the amount of your investment less any fall in its value at the
date we receive your cancellation form.**

This is a third shorter than the original. Using the active voice
has enabled other healthy writing habits to come into play.

Using 'I' or 'we' in formal reports

The myth that 'I' and 'we' should be avoided in formal reports has
crippled many writers, causing them to adopt clumsy and confusing
constructions like referring to themselves as 'the writer' or 'the
author' or using impersonal passives like 'it is thought', 'it is felt', 'it
is believed', 'it is understood' and

**It is considered that fluoridation of drinking water is beneficial to
health**

from which readers have to guess who is expressing the view: the
writer, wider scientific opinion, public opinion, or all three. In
reports, readers should not have to guess. Attempts to prohibit 'I'
and 'we' are particularly strange in that any other person, creature
or thing may be mentioned in a report.

Using personal pronouns in reports is not new. In 1877 the
British government was eager to investigate 'mechanical contrivances invented for economizing the labour of writing by hand'
and appointed a committee to 'inquire into copying machines,
departmental printing, &c'. Its report, which includes such head-

ings as 'The Type Writer', 'The Type Writer discussed', and 'Its adoption likewise advocated', regularly uses 'we' and 'our':

We have visited all the chief public Departments in London . . .

How far these objects have been satisfactorily attained, and how far such contrivances may be usefully applied in public Departments, it has been our duty to consider and report. We shall first briefly describe the various processes which have been brought under our notice.

If you are writing on your own behalf, use 'I' and 'my' judiciously, but don't overdo it for fear of seeming self-centred. If you are writing on behalf of two or more people, let 'we' and 'our' do the same job. If there is some overriding reason why these tactics are impossible, you should still make sure that most of your sentences have doers – perhaps the name of your section, department or organization.

Writers of scientific and technical material will especially benefit from using 'I' and 'we', which are becoming commonplace in many journals including the *British Medical Journal*. Unless a journal specifically prohibits these words – and most do not – you should feel free to use them. It is true that you can often omit personal pronouns by careful rewriting:

We discussed the benefits of recycling nuclear waste by home-composting methods in paragraph 3

which becomes:

Paragraph 3 discusses the benefits of recycling nuclear waste by home-composting methods.

– but the outcome is not always as neat and clear as that.

Almost everyone who writes about scientific and technical writing recommends personal pronouns. As Turk and Kirkman put it in *Effective Writing* (Spon, 1989): '. . . there is no good reason why personal pronouns should be scrupulously avoided. Readers are aware they are reading about the work of people, and their assessment of the experimental work reported will include an assessment of the personal competence of the scientist. It is artificial to avoid personal references in scientific writing.' So don't be seduced by the idea that impersonal writing makes you sound more scientific: no-one ever became a scientist by wearing a white laboratory coat.

Warning: passives can be useful

Passive verbs have their uses and it would be silly – as well as futile – for the style police to outlaw them. There are five main reasons for using them:

- To defuse hostility – actives can sometimes be too direct and blunt.
- To avoid having to say who did the action, perhaps because the doer is irrelevant or obvious from the context.
- To focus attention on the receiver of the action by putting it first – 'An 18-year-old girl has been arrested by police in connection with the Blankshire murders.'
- To spread or evade responsibility by omitting the doer, for example 'Regrettably, your file has been lost.'
- To help in positioning old or known information at the start of a sentence or clause, and new information at the end.

The last point relates to an important benefit of the passive. Read these two sentences about a nuclear reactor:

Concern has been raised about arrangements for gaining immediate access to the chimney. Winch failure or the presence of debris between the platform edge and the chimney internal wall may necessitate access.

The second sentence, written in the active voice, doesn't seem to follow from the first, whose primary focus – placed late in the sentence – is about gaining access. Now try it with the second sentence in the passive voice:

Concern has been raised about arrangements for gaining immediate access to the chimney. Access may be needed if the winch fails or there are debris between the platform edge and the chimney internal wall.

The topic of the second sentence, access, is now introduced early in that sentence and developed. There is a clear link between the focus of the first sentence and the topic of the second – a common device that helps the writing to flow by taking the reader from the known to the unknown. This is done by using the passive.

Checking your passive percentage

Manually or by using a computerized grammar checker, you can see how many passives you use. Your passive percentage is given by the formula:

100 (Number of passives ÷ number of sentences)

If you score over 50 per cent (that's one passive every two sentences) check your verbs carefully. Do you really need so many passives?

5 | Using vigorous verbs

Guideline: *Use clear, crisp, lively verbs to express the actions in your document.*

Good verbs give your writing its power and passion and delicacy. It is a simple truth that in most sentences you should express action through verbs, just as you do when you speak. Yet in so many sentences the verbs are smothered, all their vitality trapped beneath heavy noun phrases based on the smothered verbs themselves. This chapter is about releasing the power in these verbs.

Business and official writing uses plenty of smothered verbs:

- People don't *apply* for a travel pass, they make application.
- Speakers don't *inform* the public, they give information.
- Officials don't urgently *consider* a request, they give it urgent consideration.
- Staff don't *evaluate* a project, they perform an evaluation.
- Scientists don't *analyse* or *review* data, they conduct an analysis or carry out a review.
- Citizens don't *renew* their library books, they carry out a process of library book renewal.

In each case the simple verb (in italics) is being converted into a noun that needs support from another verb. The technical term for a noun that masks a verb in this way is *nominalization*. There is nothing wrong with nominalization as such – it is a useful part of the language. But overusing it tends to freeze-frame the action.

The following examples show how vigorous verbs can improve sentences containing nominalizations, making them more powerful and concise. Three types of construction are considered:

- Nominalization linked to parts of 'to be' or 'to have'.
- Nominalization linked to active verbs or infinitives.
- Nominalization linked to passive verbs.

Nominalization linked to parts of 'to be' or 'to have'

Parts of 'to be' include 'are', 'is', 'was', 'were', 'has been' and 'have been'. Parts of 'to have' include 'has', 'had' and 'have'.

Many sentences whose only verbs are parts of 'to be' or 'to have' are perfectly clear and crisp, for example:

All animals are equal, but some animals are more equal than others.

To be or not to be: that is the question.

Detailed management information is available.

In other sentences, the linking of such a verb with a nominalization is a good reason for suspecting that improvement is possible, as in this example from an official letter:

I have now had sight of your letter to Mr Jones.

The main verb is 'had' while the nominalization is 'sight', which smothers 'see'. So it would be simpler to say:

I have now <u>seen</u> your letter to Mr Jones.

This example is from a business letter:

Funding and waste management have a direct effect on progress towards the decommissioning of plant and equipment.

The main verb is 'have' while the nominalization is 'effect', which smothers 'affect'. It is crisper to write:

Funding and waste management <u>directly affect</u> progress towards the decommissioning of plant and equipment.

A combination of part of 'to be' and a nominalization is easy to see in this example:

The original intention of the researchers was to discover the state of the equipment.

The nominalization is 'intention', smothering 'intend', while 'was' acts as a prop. A revision would say:

Originally the researchers <u>intended</u> to discover the state of the equipment.

This example is from a report:

There is therefore an expectation on our part that the land will be used for building.

which becomes:

So we <u>expect</u> that the land will be used for building.

Nominalization linked to active verbs or infinitives

This construction is easy to rewrite as the presence of active verbs usually means that the word order can be preserved.

A group of conservationists is writing to a local government department:

The group considers that the director of community services should proceed with the introduction of as many mini-recycling centres as the budget allows.

The nominalization is 'introduction', propped up by 'proceed'. The rewrite would use the active voice to revive the smothered verb 'introduce':

The group considers that the director of community services should <u>introduce</u> as many mini-recycling centres as the budget allows.

A company report explains what some of the staff do:

The team's role is to perform problem definition and resolution.

Two nominalizations, 'definition' and 'resolution' are propped up by 'to perform'. Using the smothered verbs 'define' and 'resolve', this becomes:

The team's role is to <u>define</u> problems and <u>resolve</u> them.

or

The team's role is to <u>define</u> and <u>resolve</u> problems.

A government department writes:

The policy branch has carried out a review of our forms and procedures in order to effect improvements in the reporting of accidents.

Here there are two nominalizations, 'review' and 'improvements', supported by 'carried out' and 'effect' respectively. Using vigorous verbs would produce:

The policy branch <u>has reviewed</u> our forms and procedures in order <u>to improve</u> the reporting of accidents

or, putting the purpose first:

To improve the reporting of accidents, the policy branch has reviewed our forms and procedures.

It is also possible to convert noun-heavy writing into bullet-point lists. Instead of:

Meeting the new lead-in-water standards requires a combination of plumbosolvency reduction and lead pipework replacement operations

it would be simpler to write:

To meet the new lead-in-water standards we are:
- **reducing the level of dissolved lead in the water; and**
- **replacing lead pipework.**

Nominalizations linked to passive verbs

This construction is harder to revise because changing from passive to active disrupts the original word order. To compensate, however, the satisfaction is usually greater.

A housing association writes:

Notification has been received from the insurers that they wish to re-issue the Tenants Scheme Policy.

The nominalization is 'notification' and the passive is 'has been received'. Using the smothered verb 'notify' produces:

The insurers <u>have notified</u> us that they wish to re-issue the Tenants Scheme Policy.

A safety officer writes:

An examination of the maintenance records for the plant was carried out by Mr Patel.

This becomes, by the same technique:

Mr Patel <u>examined</u> the maintenance records for the plant.

When the going gets tougher

Sometimes the difficulties are harder to spot. But remember the common signals – nominalizations (often ending in -*ion*), passive voice, the verbs 'make' and 'carry out', and verbs derived from 'to be' or 'to have'.

A local government department writes:

The committee made a resolution that a study be carried out by officials into the feasibility of the provision of bottle banks in the area.

The rewriting task can be split into three operations:

1   The nominalization 'resolution' becomes a strong verb: 'The committee *resolved* that'.

2   The nominalization 'study' becomes the active verb 'study': 'officials should *study*'.

3   The nominalization 'provision' becomes a present participle (see chapter 13): 'the feasibility of *providing* bottle banks in the area'.

So the complete rewrite is:

The committee resolved that officials should study the feasibility of providing bottle banks in the area

or

The committee resolved that officials should investigate whether it is feasible to provide bottle banks in the area.

An accountant writes:

The incidence of serious monetary losses in several transactions entered into by the firm during the year is causing us great concern.

'Incidence', meaning 'rate of occurrence', isn't derived directly from a verb. Here it is probably used as a posh way of saying 'occurrence'. The real verb should be 'occur', so a rewrite could say:

The serious monetary losses that have occurred in several transactions entered into by the firm during the year are causing us great concern.

Then, reorganizing this so that the main doer comes first, the result would be:

We are very concerned about serious monetary losses in several of the firm's transactions during the year

or

The firm has lost large sums in several transactions this year, which concerns us greatly.

These word-savings would be too small a gain to justify the effort, if brevity was the only criterion. More important is that the sentences can now be read without stumbling.

6 | Using vertical lists

Guideline: *Use vertical lists to break up complicated text.*

Vertical lists have become a common feature of many documents since the 1970s, helping to present complex information in manageable chunks. For example, instead of saying this:

Our inspections will be targeted on food factories. Inspectors will investigate food factory performance, establish each occupier's performance, establish the occupier's knowledge of health and safety risks in the industry and identify which other parts of our organization could provide us with support for law enforcement

we could say this:

Our inspections will target food factories. Inspectors will:

- **investigate food factory performance;**
- **establish each occupier's performance;**
- **establish the occupier's knowledge of health-and-safety risks in the industry; and**
- **identify which other parts of our organization could give us support for law enforcement.**

Though this takes up more space it is very easy to grasp.

Vertical lists can cause problems in three areas:

- keeping the listed items in parallel;
- punctuating the listed items;
- numbering the listed items.

Let's examine each in turn.

Keeping the listed items in parallel

A dietitian is explaining how a patient should cut her salt consumption:

To restrict your salt intake, you should:

- **not add salt at the table;**
- **use only a little salt in cooking;**
- **do not use bicarbonate of soda or baking powder in cooking;**
- **avoid salty food like tinned fish, roasted peanuts, olives.**

All the listed items are understandable individually and they are all commands, so to that extent they are in parallel. But the third point doesn't fit with the lead-in or 'platform' statement. Together they are saying:

you <u>should do not use</u> bicarbonate of soda or baking powder in cooking

which is nonsense. Obviously, 'do' should be struck out to create a true parallel structure:

To restrict your salt intake, you should:
* **not add salt at the table;**
* **use only a little salt in cooking;**
* **not use bicarbonate of soda or baking powder in cooking;**
* **avoid salty food like tinned fish, roasted peanuts, olives.**

Unfortunately the job isn't complete, as there is now an odd mixture of positive and negative. The best solution might be to shift the remaining positive statement into the platform:

To restrict your salt intake, you should use only a little salt in cooking and you should not:
* **add salt at the table;**
* **use bicarbonate of soda or baking powder in cooking;**
* **eat salty food like tinned fish, roasted peanuts, olives.**

Sometimes a platform needs to be created to maintain the parallel structure. Here, a clerk is being told how to do a task:

* **You should check that the details on the self-certificate or medical certificate match those on the person's information card.**
* **You should check that the certificate has been completed correctly and conforms to the rules on validity.**
* **That the certificate covers the period of absence.**

By the third item the writer must have become tired of writing 'you should check that'. Rather than omit it, he or she should have converted it into a platform, producing:

You should check that:
* **the details on the self-certificate or medical certificate match those on the person's information card;**
* **the certificate has been completed correctly and conforms to the rules on validity;**
* **the certificate covers the period of absence.**

Often a vertical list is easier to read if each listed item has a similar grammatical structure. For example, they could all be statements that begin with infinitives or active verbs or passive verbs or present participles (see chapter 13 for explanations). In the following list, all the listed items are passive-verb statements, underlined for ease of reference:

The inspector should check that:

- **the vehicle <u>is</u> properly <u>marked</u> with hazard plates;**
- **the engine and cab heater <u>are switched off</u> during the loading and unloading of explosives;**
- **any tobacco or cigarettes <u>are kept</u> in a suitable container and matches or cigarette lighters <u>are</u> not <u>being kept</u> in the cab;**
- **the explosives <u>are</u> securely <u>stowed</u>;**

There would be no harm in adding some active-voice statements as long as they made sense when linked to the platform:

- **there are no unsecured metal objects in the vehicle's load-carrying compartments;**
- **the vehicle is carrying one or more efficient fire extinguishers.**

When statements with different grammatical structure are mixed haphazardly, the reader has to stop and backtrack. In this example, the listed items have infinitives, actives, passives or no verbs at all:

When the committee's work began, it established the following aims:

- **make the regulations simple to understand and up to date in structure and layout;**
- **to update forms and leaflets where necessary with details of current fees;**
- **the effects of competition will be considered;**
- **the creation of a document summarizing details of the regulations which will enable people to focus on key issues and requirements;**
- **recent changes in legislation should be taken into account.**

As these points are supposed to be aims, they could all be put into the infinitive:

When the committee's work began, it established the following aims:

- **<u>to</u> make the regulations simple to understand and up to date in structure and layout;**

- **to update forms and leaflets where necessary with details of current fees;**
- **to consider the effects of competition ~~will be considered~~;**
- **to create ~~the creation of~~ a document summarising details of the regulations which will enable people to focus on key issues and requirements;**
- **to take account of recent changes in legislation ~~should be taken into account~~.**

Readers get used to the pattern here; they can then concentrate better on the meaning.

Punctuating the listed items

Vertical lists need punctuating as consistently as possible so that readers get used to a pattern and are not distracted by deviations. Here is a typical example of inconsistency:

The new job-holder will:

- **develop a set of guidelines for clean wastepaper recycling**
- **Introduce green bins for clean wastepaper at appropriate places;**
- **monitor compliance with departmental targets.**

Two of the listed items begin with a lower-case letter and one with a capital. One of them ends with a semicolon, another with a full stop, and the first with nothing at all.

For greater consistency, I suggest a two-part standard.

The first part of the standard is that when a listed item is a sentence or sentence fragment that relies on the platform statement to give it meaning, it should begin with a lower-case letter and end with a semicolon – except for the final item, which should normally end with a full stop. This produces the following result:

The new job-holder will:

- **develop a set of guidelines for clean wastepaper recycling;**
- **introduce green bins for clean wastepaper at appropriate places;**
- **monitor compliance with departmental targets.**

If you wish, you could add 'and' after each of the first two semi-colons or, more conventionally, after the final semicolon only. If you wanted to show that only one of the jobs had to be done, you would put 'or' after each of the first two semicolons or, more convention-ally, after the final semicolon only:

The new job-holder will:

- **develop a set of guidelines for clean wastepaper recycling;**
- **introduce green bins for clean wastepaper at appropriate places; or**
- **monitor compliance with departmental targets.**

Alternatively you could use this kind of set-up, which stresses the 'or':

The new job-holder will:

- **develop a set of guidelines for clean wastepaper recycling;**
- or **introduce green bins for clean wastepaper at appropriate places;**
- or **monitor compliance with departmental targets.**

Rarely will you want to continue a sentence beyond a list as this could overburden the reader's short-term memory. If you do, your last listed item should end with a semicolon (though often a comma is used) and the sentence should continue with a lower-case letter:

The new job-holder will:

- **develop a set of guidelines for clean wastepaper recycling;**
- **introduce green bins for clean wastepaper at appropriate places; and**
- **monitor compliance with departmental targets;**

but the work must always take place within existing budgetary restrictions.

The second part of the standard applies to listed items that are complete sentences and don't depend on the platform statement to give them meaning. These should begin with a capital and end with a full stop. For example:

The speaker made three points:

- **Aboriginal people across the world have been persecuted in the name of civilisation and religion.**
- **Even so-called enlightened governments have broken treaties made in good faith by aboriginals.**
- **Despair among aboriginals will lead either to their cultural disintegration or uprisings against authority.**

This treatment is particularly useful when a listed item is long and detailed, perhaps with several separate sentences, as it would seem odd if the listed item began with a lower-case letter, went on with a new sentence, and ended in a semicolon.

Normally it is not enough to end listed items with a comma or no punctuation at all, though this is often done. The signal is not strong enough: a semicolon or full stop gives more warning of a major break. No standard, however, can apply in every case and there may be times when you need to deviate from it – especially if you want the text to have the clean and very informal look that absence of punctuation (or just a final full stop) can bring.

Numbering the listed items

There is no need to number the listed items if you or the reader will not need to refer to them again or if you wish to avoid suggesting that the items are in order of priority. Instead, just use a dash followed by a space, or a 'bullet' •.

Other options are arabic numbers (1, 2, 3) or bracketed letters (a), (b), (c) or, as a last resort, bracketed roman numerals (i), (ii), (iii). Roman numerals can be used if you need to put a list within a list – more common in legal documents than in everyday writing:

> **The court may in an order made by it in relation to a regulated agreement include provisions:**
>
>   (a) **making the operation of any term of the order conditional on the doing of specified acts by any party;**
>   (b) **suspending the operation of any term of the order:**
>   (i) **until the court subsequently directs; or**
>   (ii) **until the occurrence of a specified act or omission.**

Seeing the possibility for vertical lists

Sometimes the only method of enlivening and clarifying a piece of dreary text is a vertical list, so you need to be alive to the possibility. The following example is the first part of a local authority's information leaflet to students explaining whether they are entitled to some money:

> **Maintenance grants when studying abroad**
>
> *Students of modern languages*
>
> **A student of modern languages is defined by the regulations as a student whose course 'includes the study of one or more modern languages other than English for not less than half of the time spent studying the course and which includes periods of residence in a country whose language is a main language of the course'.**

This seems at first to be beyond improvement – it is almost a straight quote from a regulation so a paraphrase may be troublesome. Yet if you examine it from the reader's viewpoint, hope begins to emerge. You can see that the focus should really be on the effect of the regulations on the student, not on what the regulations say, while 'includes' is used twice, suggesting the possibility of a vertical list. Using these levers, you can personalize the information, switch it into question-and-answer style, and introduce a list. Through a bit of trial and error, you can produce something like this before getting your in-house lawyers to check it for accuracy:

Maintenance grants when studying abroad

Who can get a maintenance grant?

You can get a grant if you are a student of modern languages. According to the regulations, this means that your course must include both:

- **the study of one or more modern languages (except English) for at least half the course time; and**

- **periods of residence in a country whose language is a main language of the course.**

7 | Negative to positive

Guideline: *Put your points positively when you can.*

'Accentuate the positive, eliminate the negative,' went the old song. In writing, negatives include 'un-' words like 'unnecessary' and 'unless'; verbs with negative associations like 'avoid' and 'cease'; and the obvious ones like 'not', 'no', 'except', 'less than', 'not less than' and 'not more than'. When readers are faced with a negative, they must first imagine the positive alternative then mentally cancel it out. So when a newspaper declares:

> It is surely less painful to be unemployed if one is not sober, drug-free and filled with a desire to work

readers have to work very hard to assemble the meaning.

A single negative is unlikely to cause problems, though many a British voter has paused, pen poised, when confronted with the polling-booth challenge:

> Vote for not more than one candidate

instead of the plainer and positive:

> Vote for one candidate only.

But when two, three or more negatives are gathered together in the same sentence, meaning may become obscure, as in this note from a lawyer to his client, an underwriter:

> Underwriters are, we consider, free to form the view that James Brothers have <u>not yet proved</u> to their satisfaction that the short-landed bags were <u>not discharged</u> from the ship, and were <u>not lost</u> in transit between Antwerp and Dieppe, when they were <u>not covered</u> by this insurance policy

– a rodeo ride that perhaps only the lawyer who created it could negotiate without falling off. The going is a little easier here in a pension contract:

> 'Dependant relative' includes a member's child or adopted child who has <u>not attained</u> the age of 18 or has <u>not ceased</u> to receive full-time education or training.

Put positively this would say:

'Dependant relative' includes a member's child or adopted child who is <u>aged 17 or under</u> or is in full-time education or training.

Just as 'at least' is an ever-present help in a document full of not-less-thans, the word 'only' – which is positive but restrictive – is a useful converter of negative to positive:

The government will not consent to an application if those with a legal interest in the common land object to the application, except in exceptional circumstances.

'Not' and 'unless' both vanish under the influence of 'only':

Only in exceptional circumstances will the government consent to an application if those with a legal interest in the common land object to the application

or

If those with a legal interest in the common land object to an application, the government will consent to it only in exceptional circumstances.

This note was sent to a parent of a child with special needs (learning difficulties) by a local education authority:

It is unusual for us not to be able to find a place for a child with special needs in one of our schools.

People can easily misinterpret the double negative as a single negative and think it means 'We cannot usually . . .', especially if they are used to getting negative replies from authority figures. The intended meaning, of course, is positive:

We can usually find a place for a child with special needs in one of our schools.

Some bureaucracies seem addicted to elaborate negativity:

I see no reason why the firm should not require properly prepared supporting bills. (Meaning: 'It is reasonable for the firm to ask you for proper receipts.')

The authority's actions do not appear to be unreasonable in the circumstances. (Meaning: 'The authority seems to have acted reasonably.')

It is difficult to say what, if any, difference this information would have made to the councillors' assessment of your request. However, I do not believe I can safely say that it would definitely have made no difference. (Meaning: 'I don't know whether this information would have affected the councillors' assessment, but it might have done.')

Clearly there can be a difference in meaning between an action being 'not unreasonable' and just plain 'reasonable'. But always ask yourself whether such distinctions are worth making in the particular case.

Rules from the European Commission are a fertile source of multiple negatives, as in this 67-word sentence from, ironically, a regulation on public access to documents (EC1049/2001):

> Even though it is neither the object nor the effect of this Regulation to amend national legislation on access to documents, it is nevertheless clear that, by virtue of the principle of loyal cooperation which governs relations between the institutions and the Member States, Member States should take care not to hamper the proper application of this Regulation and should respect the security rules of the institutions

– which, with fewer negatives and a vertical list, could become:

> This Regulation does not amend or seek to amend national legislation on access to documents. Yet the principle of loyal cooperation that governs relations between the institutions and the Member States means that Member States should:
>
> > (a) take care not to hamper the proper application of this Regulation; and
> >
> > (b) respect the security rules of the institutions.

Negatives are, of course, useful. Many commands are more powerful in the negative, which is why they have a place in procedures and instruction manuals. Even a double negative like:

> Do not switch on the power unless you have made all the necessary checks

is probably more forceful than:

> Only switch on the power when you have made the necessary checks.

But avoid overusing negatives, and make sure that those you use are necessary.

8 | Cross-references, cross readers

Guideline: *Reduce cross-references to a minimum.*

The British government has sent me a 26-page form that includes 183 questions, 70 separate paragraphs of notes and about 125 cross-references from questions to notes. A tax schedule to the Finance No 2 Act of 1992 includes about 40 internal cross-references, forwards and backwards. In both cases, I am whizzed from point to point like a pinball from the flippers.

In any complex document some cross-references are inevitable but they should be kept to the minimum. Unless they are carefully controlled, this kind of horror from a pension policy is the likely result:

> In the event of the policyholder being alive on the vesting date and having given (or being deemed to have given) appropriate notice in accordance with provision 11.4 the provisions set out in this provision 5 shall apply provided that where by reason of the policyholder's exercise of the option under provision 6.2 or 6.3 the vesting date is a day which is not the specified date, provision 5 shall apply subject to any consequential alterations arising under the relevant part of provision 6.

Plain English can't improve this very much. The only hope is to scrap it and start again. If the point can't be made in a way that people can understand, it may not be worth making at all: the scheme underlying the policy might need to be simplified.

Skeins of cross-references are not always so hopelessly tangled. Here's an example from an investment policy:

> If you choose to receive income payments from your investment within the policy, subject as provided in clause 12, income (including tax credits) will be paid to you (subject to such sums being available first to pay any sums due to Unicorn Unit Trusts Limited under clause 9) monthly or quarterly and at any level you choose between a minimum of 5 per cent and a maximum of 10 per cent (in increments of 0.5 per cent) based on either a percentage of your original

investment or the value of your policy at the time you choose to start making withdrawals.

To isolate and jot down the main points in this 98-word sentence is not easy. But it will go a long way towards clearing up the mess:

1 If you have chosen to draw income from the investment, we will pay it to you, monthly or quarterly.

2 How much we pay you could be affected by clause 12 and by Unicorn's charges set out in clause 9.

3 We will pay you whatever percentage you choose – within certain limits – of your original investment or of the value of your investment at the time you start to make withdrawals.

By putting these points in 1–3–2 order, the cross-references can be grouped into a separate sentence at the end. The result might say this, using short sentences and paragraphs:

If you choose to draw income payments from your investment in the policy, we will pay them to you monthly or quarterly. The payments will include tax credits.

The payments you choose must be a percentage of your original investment or of the value of your investment at the time you start receiving the income. Your choice of percentage must be at least 5 per cent but not more than 10 per cent (using 0.5 per cent steps).

Payments are subject to clause 12 and are available first to pay any money owed to Unicorn Unit Trusts Limited under clause 9.

This is still not simple because the ideas themselves are complicated and, though there are fewer words, they take more space. But now readers have a much better chance of understanding the points, and can ask sensible questions if they need more information.

9 | Clearly non-sexist

Guideline: *Try to avoid sexist usage.*

Trying to sell cat litter through posters on the London underground may not be easy, and since many cats are owned by women, the task becomes harder if the wording of the posters excludes them:

> **Keep your fur on. Your owner is as concerned with hygiene as you are, which is why he buys Catsan Hygiene Cat Litter . . . In fact, Catsan works so well that it actually produces less odour after six days than ordinary cat litters do after only one day . . . Which means your owner will have to change it less often. Allowing them to get on with their life and you to get on with yours, all nine of them.**

Though sexist usage is not strictly a matter of clarity, any writing habit that builds a barrier between you and half your readers must reduce the impact of your message. So even if you disagree with the view that sexist writing reinforces prejudice and discrimination, it is still wiser to use inclusive language. Occasional silliness apart ('the art of one-upping' doesn't have quite the same ring as 'one-upmanship'), inclusive writing usually makes more sense and more accurately reflects reality.

Using sex-neutral terms

Using sex-neutral terms means avoiding words suggesting that maleness is the norm or superior or positive and that femaleness is non-standard, subordinate or negative. Sex-specific terms like 'businessmen', 'firemen', 'poetess', 'headmaster' and 'sculptress' can be replaced by less restrictive words: 'business people' (or 'executives'), 'firefighters', 'poet', 'headteacher' and 'sculptor'. Some sex-specific terms may survive this trend, such as 'actress' – which perhaps lacks some of the negative echoes of low status and low pay – though some actresses specifically refer to themselves as 'actors'. 'Fishers' and 'fisherfolk' seem unlikely to gain popular acceptance as alternatives to 'fishermen' on the open sea, yet 'anglers' is a convenient sex-neutral term for those who fish for sport. There seem not to be any palatable alternatives for such terms as 'manned

space flight' and 'craftsmanship'. The British socialist Barbara
Castle once said she didn't mind whether people called her chair,
chairman or chairwoman as long as she was in the chair.

Sex-specific words	Sex-neutral words
authoress	author
aviatrix	aviator
chairman, chairwoman	chair (or ask what they prefer)
clergymen	clergy, clerics
comedienne	comedian
craftsmen	craft workers, artisans
executrix	executor
forelady, foreman	supervisor, head juror (law)
heroine	hero
layman	lay person
man, mankind (humans)	the human species, human beings, people, humans, humanity
man (noun)	person, individual, you
man (verb)	operate, staff, run, work
manageress	manager
man-hours	working hours, work-hours
man-made	manufactured, artificial
parliamentary draftsman	parliamentary counsel/drafter
policeman, policewoman	police officer
salesman, salesgirl	sales agent/representative/ consultant
testatrix	testator, will-maker
workman	worker

Using titles or 'he or she'

It is better to avoid 'he', 'his' or 'him' when you intend to include
both men and women. Instead of:

**Solvent abuse is not a crime but if a police officer finds a young
person under 17 sniffing solvents, he should take him to a secure
place such as a police station, home or hospital**

you could repeat the short titles of both people:

Solvent abuse is not a crime but if a police officer finds a young person under 17 sniffing solvents, <u>the officer</u> should take <u>the person</u> to a secure place such as home, a police station or a hospital.

Using 'he or she' and 'him or her' is also feasible here – perhaps, to avoid confusion, for just one of the people:

Solvent abuse is not a crime but if a police officer finds a person under 17 sniffing solvents, <u>he or she</u> should take the person to a secure place such as home, a police station or a hospital.

Repeated use of 'he or she' and similar terms becomes clumsy and obtrusive. The alternatives, 's/he' or 'he/she', look ugly and cannot be spoken easily.

In guidance to police officers, it would be feasible to use 'you':

Solvent abuse is not a crime but if <u>you</u> find a person under 17 sniffing solvents, <u>you</u> should take <u>him or her</u> to a secure place such as his or her home, a police station or a hospital.

In a booklet issued to parents about schools, one British local education authority gets round the problem neatly by referring to 'your child' as 'he' on odd-numbered pages and 'she' on even-numbered pages. This fix is explained in the introduction.

Using the plural

A further alternative, and often the best, is to use the plural:

Solvent abuse is not a crime but if <u>police officers</u> find a person under 17 sniffing solvents, <u>they</u> should take the person to a secure place such as the person's home, a police station or a hospital.

Using the plural helps to disentangle difficulties such as this:

If the court grants immediate possession, the tenant and anyone else living with him or her is required to leave his, her or their home immediately. If he, she or they do not do so, the court bailiffs will evict him, her or them but there is usually a delay before this happens.

This could become:

If the court grants immediate possession, the tenant and anyone living with them must leave their home immediately. If they do not do so, the court bailiff will evict them but there is usually a delay before this happens

or, with further gymnastics:

If the court grants immediate possession, the tenant must leave his or her home. If the tenant does not do so, the court bailiff will evict him or her. The same applies to anyone living with the tenant.

Using plurals as singulars

It is becoming more acceptable to flout the grammatical conventions set in the eighteenth century by male grammarians and to do what Shakespeare did when he wrote:

God send everyone their heart's desire.

In other words, to revive the old use of 'they', 'them' and 'their' as singulars, as in these examples from forms and standard letters:

1 **Give details of your partner's income. If <u>they</u> have been unemployed for more than 12 months . . .**

2 **Your child has been chosen to take part in a class to further support and consolidate <u>their</u> creative writing skills.**

3 **You may find that an individual has levels of competence in several skills beyond those required in <u>their</u> current role. This will occur when the person has developed <u>their</u> skills and potential in readiness for other opportunities.**

To me, these read smoothly enough, though the third might be better wholly in the plural:

You may find that <u>individuals</u> have levels of competence in several skills beyond those required in their current roles. This will occur when <u>they</u> have developed their skills and potential in readiness for other opportunities.

'Everybody' and 'everyone' are clearly singular in appearance but for centuries have often been followed by a plural pronoun in speech and writing, which avoids the need for 'his/her':

Every one Sacrifices a Cow or more, according to their different Degrees of Wealth or Devotion. (Dr Johnson, 1735 – note the now-strange capitalization and ancient split of 'Every one')

Everyone was absorbed in their own businesses. (Andrew Motion, now poet laureate, 1989)

Every body does and says what they please. (Byron, 1820)

Everybody seems to recover their spirits. (John Ruskin, 1866)

Everybody has a right to describe their own party machine as they choose. (Winston Churchill, 1954)

It is worth remembering that using the plural as a singular still infuriates some diehards. If you can sensibly avoid it, do.

Postscript: the alternatives are worse

To reject all the ideas as bad compromises means accepting the kind of writing found in this advert from the 1920s, in which all typists are assumed to be women and all managers men:

By dictating [. . .] you enable your typist to be typing all day, not wasting half the morning taking notes [. . .] She writes more letters and does her work more easily and accurately. Also the Dictaphone saves the time of the chief. We hardly like to talk about the 'after-hours' work, but it is acknowledged that closing time is the time when men who bear the real burdens oftentimes get down to their serious work. Then is the time when a man can concentrate, when there are no interruptions, no clicking of typewriters, no buzz of conversation to disturb his train of thought. Minds become decisive, delicate situations are mastered, and tactful, forceful phrases find shape. Here it is that the Dictaphone comes into its own; it records the accumulated letters for the typist first thing in the morning, the chief's desk is clear – his mind relieved, and he arrives next day with only the 'current' matter to receive his attention.

As late as 1998, I found this example in an in-company report written by a female middle manager:

He asked me to speak to Jane and Alice. I asked the girls if they had been using the business transfer form supplied during my previous visit. They said they had. Michael asked the girls to think of the names of some of the policies that should be on the quarterly list. The girls agreed, then left the room.

Modern business practice is to give Jane and Alice surnames when they are first mentioned, then to use 'them', 'they, 'his assistants' or 'Jane and Alice'. If this seems pernickety, try inserting male forenames and 'boys' at the appropriate places. 'Boys' and 'girls' are widely regarded as demeaning terms in the workplace.

10 | Sound starts and excellent endings

Guideline: *In letters, avoid fusty first sentences and formula finishes.*

In letters and memos the best place to start being straightforward is at the beginning. Your first sentence should be clear, complete, concise and written in modern English. This is easily done if you steer clear of three common traps.

Trap 1: Writing half a sentence instead of a full one

All these first sentences are incomplete:

> Further to your letter of 3 February concerning the trustees of the P F Smith 1982 Settlement.

> With reference to our previous correspondence notifying you of the transfer of the administration of the above policy to Norwich Union Healthcare with effect from 9 January.

> In response to your letter to Mr Jones dated 19 February.

> Regarding your claim for attendance allowance.

> Referring to your letter dated 10 July about delayed frequency allocations.

Each statement needs to be continued and completed, inserting a comma instead of a full stop. For example:

> Further to your letter of 3 February concerning the trustees of the P F Smith 1982 Settlement, I am pleased to enclose the form you requested.

> Regarding your claim for attendance allowance, I need to ask you for some more information.

Alternatively, you could insert a main verb at the start to complete the sentences:

Thank you for your letter of 3 February concerning the trustees of the P F Smith 1982 Settlement.

I refer to your claim for attendance allowance.

Other verbs that will do a similar job include 'I acknowledge'; 'I confirm'; 'I write to explain'. These alternatives are preferable for another reason: they use personal words like 'I', 'you' and 'we'.

Don't be afraid to write a one-sentence paragraph at the start of a letter:

Thank you for your letter dated 13 May.

If you are taking the initiative – rather than responding to someone's enquiry – these phrases may be helpful to get your first sentence off to a sound start:

You are warmly invited to . . .

You may be interested in . . .

This is an opportunity to . . .

Now is a good time to consider . . .

Or you could ask a question – preferably one to which the reader will answer yes:

Does your office have old and outdated law books gathering dust in corners? Would you like to create some extra space for yourself, and see those books go to a good cause at the same time? If so . . .

Trap 2: Repeating the heading

Most business and official letters benefit from a heading, as it introduces the topic and saves having to write a long first sentence to cover the same ground. The heading (usually underlined or in bold type) might even run to several lines:

Curtis Brothers Ltd
Lease Agreement No. 727-252-8978
Goods: Touchtone Telephone System
Installation address: Piller House, Crook Street, Downtown

Whether the heading is short or long, don't keep referring to it with such phrases as 'with reference to the above-mentioned equipment', 'regarding the above-numbered agreement', 'the above matter' and 'in connection with the aforementioned'. Let's say you are selling property and someone has phoned for details of a house. Instead of writing:

Dear Ms Widdicombe

'The Tree House', 67 Larch Avenue, Poplar

I refer to your enquiry yesterday in relation to the above-mentioned property, and enclose details as requested

it is crisper to write:

Dear Ms Widdicombe

'The Tree House', 67 Larch Avenue, Poplar

I refer to your enquiry yesterday and enclose details of the property as requested

or

Thank you for your enquiry yesterday about this property; details are enclosed

or

Thank you for your enquiry. I am pleased to enclose details of this spacious and well-situated house.

This last suggestion has the advantage of mentioning some of the key selling points immediately.

Trap 3: Archaic usage

Avoid fusty usage like:

Our recent telephone discussion <u>refers</u>.

Modern readers find 'refers' very odd in this position. Use 'I refer to . . .' or 'In our recent telephone conversation, we discussed . . .'. In an internal document you could merely say 'We spoke about this.', when the heading will provide enough context for what you spoke about.

Just as fusty is:

<u>Re</u> your letter of the 10th, <u>the contents of which have been noted</u>.

'Re' is Latin for 'in the matter of' and is best avoided. When responding to someone's letter it is stating the obvious to say that you have 'noted the contents'. And anyway, the phrase sounds bureaucratic and disapproving – avoid it. Similarly, avoid 'instant', 'ultimo' and 'proxime', which some writers still use to mean 'this month', 'last month' and 'next month' respectively, for example:

Thank you for your letter of the 15th instant.

Finishing well

Keep the finish simple and sincere. In a sales letter you could reiterate an important action point:

I look forward to receiving your application soon, then you can begin to benefit from all our services.

You could even add a PS beneath the signature. Useful non-selling sign-offs include 'I hope this is helpful' (which is much better than the negative and servile 'I am sorry I cannot be more helpful'); and 'If you need more information, please contact me' (which is better than waffle like 'Should you require any further assistance or clarification from ourselves with regard to this matter, please do not hesitate to contact the writer undersigned').

If you are trying to close a correspondence with a difficult customer, you could try:

I hope you will understand our position, and I regret that we cannot help any further.

If a complainant won't take no for an answer and you cannot help any further, you can try:

Unless you provide any new information about this matter, I regret that we will not respond to your letters.

Remember: these are only suggestions. Compose your own phrases to suit your own circumstances and personality. Make it sound individually crafted if you can.

Conventions on opening and closing

If you start with 'Dear [first name]', 'Dear [Mr/Mrs/Miss/Ms]', or 'Dear [first name and surname]', the conventional endings are 'Yours sincerely', 'Sincerely yours' or 'Yours truly'. Alternatively, use a sensible sign-off of your own making: 'Kind regards' and 'Best wishes' are now common among people well known to each other. 'Regards' and 'kind regards' are common in informal and semi-formal e-mails.

If you begin 'Dear Sir' or 'Dear Madam', the traditional formal ending is 'Yours faithfully' or, in the US, 'Yours truly'. An alternative opening is to use the organization's name: 'Dear Express Bus Company.'

In British English, the 'Dear . . .' salutation is followed by a comma or nothing. Whichever is used, the pattern is repeated after the 'Yours . . .' closure. In American English, the salutation is usually followed by a colon (formal) or comma (informal) and the closure by a comma.

Esquires were originally the shield-bearers of knights, or men in royal or noble service. Once a favoured courtesy title after a man's name, 'Esq' is now rarely seen in the address block of a letter. It is perhaps thought over-formal or servile. The title is not applied to a woman's name except, oddly, among US lawyers, where both sexes use it when writing to each other. Nor does it traditionally follow 'Mr', so 'Mr J Smith Esq' is unusual.

Punctuation can be slashed from the address block in British English (though it's still common in the US), so this:

J. H. Author, Esq.,
34, Ivory Lane,
Kelvintown,
KT2 0NN.

becomes:

Mr J H Author
34 Ivory Lane
Kelvintown
KT2 0NN

In the UK, with its complicated honours system and welter of titles for royalty, the peerage and religious office-holders, the usually simple jobs of addressing an envelope, greeting a correspondent and closing a letter can be hazardous. If your work requires you to write to peers and the like, you will find a helpful path charted for you (and as much feudal wisdom as you can stomach) in the 197 pages of *Titles and Forms of Address* (A&C Black, 2002) and the 375 pages of *Debrett's Correct Form* (Headline, 1999).

11 | Using good punctuation

Guideline: *Put accurate punctuation at the heart of your writing.*

Punctuation shouldn't cause as much fear as it does. Only about a dozen marks need to be mastered and the guidelines are fairly simple. What's more, you can see the marks being well applied every day in the newspapers, where 99 per cent of the punctuation will accord with the advice given here. Study of press punctuation also reveals the full range of marks, as journalists – especially the star columnists – use far more colons, semicolons and dashes than business and official writers.

The rumour has got about that any old punctuation, or none at all, will do. This is as bad a fallacy as saying that any old words in any old order will do, as long as the readers can pick up the general idea. A good command of punctuation helps you to say more, say it more interestingly and exactly, and be understood at first reading. Punctuation is an essential part of the tool-kit – as important as choosing the right words.

Consider these statements:

Mother to be attacked on waste land.

Never mind people who dislike cats are in a minority.

Once she had the dress off she would go in search of matching shoes, gloves and a handbag.

Without good punctuation they can be interpreted in different ways or make no sense at all, distracting the readers and causing them to stop and backtrack. Punctuation helps to fix the meaning and smooth the path:

Mother-to-be attacked on waste land.

Never mind: people who dislike cats are in a minority.

Once she had the dress, off she would go in search of matching shoes, gloves and a handbag.

Punctuation shows how words and strings of words are related, separated and emphasized, so its main purpose is to help the reader understand the construction of the sentence. A lesser purpose is to act as a substitute for the devices we all use in speech, such as pausing and altering pitch; but an idea such as 'use a comma when you would have a one-beat pause in speech, a semicolon for a two-beat pause, and a full stop for a three-beat pause' is unhelpful because it can be interpreted in too many ways. Even so, you might want to read a sentence aloud to help you decide how to punctuate it.

Though this chapter describes the standards that most careful writers accept as sound, no two writers will ever agree on the position of every comma and full stop. So if you are editing someone's writing, be prepared for a bit of give and take.

Today, even careful writers have to face the fact that fine distinctions between such marks as colons and semicolons will be lost on many of their readers. Yet so long as readers regard a semicolon as a funny-looking comma and a colon as a bit like a full stop, that will usually give them enough to hang on to. So, even if you decide to use the less common punctuation marks sparingly when writing for a mass audience, there is no need to remove them altogether.

After a period when the teaching of punctuation seemed unfashionable in some British schools, children in the early twenty-first century are again learning the main rules. From the age of six or seven, they are also reading books showing the full range of marks, as in *The Green Cushion* by Margaret Joy: 'Let me think,' said Old Joey. 'Charlie from the chippy took one. Mrs Tomkins took one – she lives over at number nineteen; and Miss Wilson took the third one – she lives opposite at Rose Villa.'

Full stop (.)

As shown in chapter 1, the main use of a full stop (or, in the US, period) is to show where a sentence ends. For this reason, full stops should be the most common mark on the page.

There's no need to use full stops in people's names or in abbreviations or acronyms – *Mr J C Bennett, BBC, US, eg, ie, 8am, 9pm* – unless there's a genuine chance of ambiguity. Headings in a report, letter, e-mail or memo don't need a final full stop.

Comma (,)

Single commas act as separators between parts of a sentence:

Using accident and ill-health data and drawing upon my experience of inspecting slaughterhouses and meat-processing plants, I have prepared a list of hazards found in the meat industry

or:

Although suitable protective equipment was available, most of the operatives were not wearing it

or:

If you send the documents by Thursday, we will complete the sale by the following Monday.

Be sparing with commas. Using them every few words may prevent the reader getting the construction of the sentence. This, for example, is a mess:

I have tried on a number of occasions to contact you at your office, without success and now resort, to writing to you, as these items should be dealt with urgently. You will appreciate the possible problems involved, if these units become occupied, before we have had a chance to check for their compliance with standards, and I would be obliged, if you could respond, by complying with my inspector's original request for compliance, as any further delay, could result in the start of disciplinary action against your company.

Almost every comma could go and the long final sentence could be split.

A pair of commas cordons off information that is an aside, explanation or addition. Readers can, if they wish, leapfrog the cordoned-off area and still make sense of what is said:

Holmes, having searched for further clues, left by the back door.

Often the position of commas will change the meaning, so be careful with them:

The girls, who will join the team next week, are fine players for their age.

Here, the information between the commas comments on 'the girls', but is not essential to the main point of the sentence, which is that the girls are fine players. This kind of insert is said to be a commenting clause. Compare this, without commas:

The girls who will join the team next week are fine players for their age.

Obviously the meaning has changed: the words 'who will join the team next week' now help to define the girls. They are essential to our understanding of what kind of people they are. The clause is said to be defining and does not need a cordon of commas.

Commas are helpful in separating listed items:

Staple foods include rice, wheat, sorghum and millet.

No comma is needed after *sorghum* (though it is usual in US English), but when the penultimate or final listed item includes *and*, a comma in the right place can help the reader to see the meaning immediately:

To get an award, you must obtain a pass on theory, practical knowledge, and health and safety.

A comma can also help to create special effects like suspense. Compare this:

They crept into the room and found the body

with:

They crept into the room, and found the body.

Finally, ignore the advice often heard on writing courses: 'Use a maximum of one comma per sentence.' It is just plain silly.

Colon (:)

A colon is used to introduce direct speech, as an alternative to a comma; and to separate a main heading from a subtitle, as in 'Elephants: the full facts'. Colons have three other main purposes:

1   To introduce a vertical list (as in the line above) or a running-text list where there is a substantial break after the introductory phrase, such as:

    She has several positive characteristics: charm, dignity and stickability.

    For notes on the punctuation of vertical lists, see chapter 6.

2   To act as a drum roll (mark of announcement) or a 'why-because' marker that leads the reader from one idea to its consequence or logical continuation, for example:

    There's one big problem with tennis on radio: you can't see it.

3 Much more rarely, to separate two sharply contrasting and parallel statements as in the example always quoted in punctuation guides, 'Man proposes: God disposes.' Here is a more secular colon:

During Wimbledon, television is like someone with a reserved ticket: radio is the enthusiast who has queued all night to get in.

A weaker contrast might be signified by a semicolon; there is some overlap in meaning between the two marks.

In all these uses, the colon will usually follow a statement that could be a complete sentence. After the colon the sentence will usually continue with a lower-case letter.

A colon does not need support from a dash (:–). This nameless thing is not acceptable to most publishers, wastes a key stroke, and looks repulsive in most word-processed documents.

Semicolon (;)

Consider these sentences from a notice next to an ancient cathedral clock:

The large oak frame houses the striking train of gears, these parts have been painted black and are the early parts of the clock. In this same frame on the left between two posts is a going train (a time piece), this has been painted green.

Both commas are wrong and should be semicolons or full stops. To use semicolons safely – ignoring for the moment their use in lists – you need to satisfy two criteria:

1 The statements separated by the semicolons could stand alone as separate sentences.

2 The topics mentioned in the two statements are closely related.

So the paragraph would say:

The large oak frame houses the striking train of gears; these parts have been painted black and are the early parts of the clock. In this same frame on the left between two posts is a going train (a time piece); this has been painted green.

A semicolon can often seem less curt than a full stop. Instead of starting a letter:

Thank you for your letter of 10 December. We apologize for the delay in replying

it would be better to write:

Thank you for your letter of 10 December; we apologize for the delay in replying.

A comma would be wrong in that position because it cannot sustain such a long pause. Rarely is a comma enough to separate complete sentences.

Semicolons can also be used instead of commas to separate items in a list:

Lunch at Henry's comprised all the ingredients for a happy and contented life: wine from the grapes of Tuscany; tropical avocados, seductively soft and yielding; French king prawns, clothed in a luscious sauce; a multitude of meaty snacks for carnivores and nutty nibbles for vegetarians; and the company of all the beautiful people of the town.

In a long, catalogue-type list, semicolons are ideal dividers:

Target audiences for the new manual will include other companies in our group, both European and US-based; business leaders, top politicians and other leading opinion-formers; consultants of proven expertise; and local schools and colleges.

To use merely commas as dividers would produce chaos because commas already exist within some of the listed items. An introductory colon after include would be unnecessary – there is no substantial pause at that point.

Dash (–)

Dashes are sometimes used singly to indicate the start of an aside, explanation or addition:

Justifying their case, smokers introduce a herring so red that it glows like coal: that if their illnesses are self-inflicted, well, so are most people's – look at traffic accidents, look at potholers.

They can add emphasis, too:

He shot big game for status, pleasure – and greed.

When used in pairs, dashes draw special attention to the phrase they surround (compare 'Brackets', below):

Visitors may stay overnight – or for as long as they wish – in the hostelry run by the friars.

A pair of commas or a pair of brackets would have done just as well, but the dashes emphasize the point.

It is all right to use more than one pair of dashes in a sentence but take care that the meaning doesn't disintegrate. Here's an awkward, if playful, use of two pairs of dashes by a newspaper columnist:

Volkswagen is in trouble – terrible trouble – very terrible trouble, and we can sit on the sidelines – entry free – and bask in somebody else's trouble for hours on end.

Perhaps he should have read his paper's own guide on the subject of dashes:

Dashes are sloppy punctuation, ugly in narrow columns of newspaper type. They often indicate that a sentence is badly constructed and needs rewriting.

Happily this advice is ignored by everyone on the paper.

In typewriting, where dashes are not usually available, it is customary to use a hyphen (or, more rarely, double hyphen) with a space either side. In typesetting or desk-top publishing, most publishers use a spaced 'en rule' – which is what I have just used.

The en rule (or en dash) is not obvious on most keyboards but may be an option under the hyphen key. Some publishers use an 'em rule' (or em dash), which is slightly longer than the en rule, for all the purposes described above. An unspaced en rule is often used to show a range of dates or other figures, eg '1958–2004' or 'rats aged 6–9 months were used in the experiment'.

Brackets ( )

Brackets (also called round brackets or, in the US, parentheses) surround an aside, explanation or addition that is relatively unimportant to the main text (compare 'Dash', above):

The biker fell off at 160 mph, suffering an open fracture of his tibia (lower leg) and losing two inches of bone in the process. Only ten years ago, four out of ten open tibial fractures (in which the bone comes partially out of the leg) resulted in amputation.

Well-placed brackets can prevent the meaning of a sentence disintegrating, even if the result looks cluttered:

The problem is tidal flooding along the river. Many plans have been studied but the agreed solution is a system of river mattressing (to avoid breaches) and embankment raising (to avoid exceptionally high-tide flooding).

If a sentence begins within a bracket, it should start with a capital and end with a full stop inside the bracket. A comma should rarely precede a bracket but there is no harm in putting one after the closing bracket if this aids understanding.

If you are going to use an acronym several times and the reader is unlikely to know what it means, spell it out on the first occasion and put the acronym in brackets:

Agency Services Limited (ASL) has tendered for the work.

Other types of bracket are brace or curly brackets {which are used in maths} and angle brackets <used in linguistics and other specialisms>.

Square brackets [ ]

Square brackets (or, in the US, brackets) show that the text within does not belong to the document or quotation but is being inserted for clarity:

He [Mr Smith] told me to go home.

They saw it [the pheasant] as fair game.

Capitals

Capital letters (upper case) defy any would-be rule-maker, as some decisions on whether to dignify a word with an initial capital have to be left to the individual writer. Use them sparingly though, and err on the side of lower case. Writing afflicted with random capitalitis just looks silly:

Please Complete One Line For Each Person Normally Living At This Address, including those who are temporarily living away. Include Everybody – Yourself, All Adults, whether entered or not on the Electoral Registration form, All Younger Persons, Children and Babies.

Headings in business and scientific reports tend to suffer from the same disease, with writers making invidious distinctions between words they capitalize and words they don't. Compare the distracting:

Factors that May Affect the Success of the Strategy

with:

Factors that may affect the success of the strategy.

In the US, headings in books often use 'title case', where the initial letters of nouns and adjectives (and sometimes even verbs) are capitalized. Title case spills over into reports and letters and, under the influence of Microsoft Word, is often seen in UK documents. It lends a rather self-important impression, especially when applied to all the subheadings as well as chapter or section headings. It also gives an inconsistent look because words in lower case in the main text suddenly assume a higher status in headings.

People: Use an initial capital for ranks and titles when attached to a person's name, thus *Prince William* but *the prince*, *President Bush* but *the president*, *Judge Wright* but *the judge*. Offices of state in the UK such as *home secretary* and *chancellor of the exchequer* are lower case in *The Economist* and *The Sunday Times*, but become *Home Secretary* and *Chancellor of the Exchequer* in *The Times*. I prefer lower case. Titles that look odd in lower case need capitalizing, hence *Master of the Rolls*, *Lord Chief Justice*. In some organizations, job titles like *managing director* are given initial capitals but this is poor practice – at what rank do you stop? It helps if the organization issues a style guide setting out its house rules.

Organizations, acts of Parliament and government departments generally take initial capitals only when their full name or something similar is used. Thus *Metropolitan Police* but *the police*; *County Court* and *Court of Appeal* but *the court*; *the Health and Safety at Work etc Act* but *the act*; *Legal Services Commission* but *legal aid*. A newspaper would usually print *Blankshire District Council* but *the council*. The council itself, however, might prefer to use a capital c whenever it referred to itself. Confusion sets in when it then refers to another council, to which it will invariably give a lower-case letter. The result is an apparent inconsistency, and the main merit of a general preference for lower case is that it tends to produce a much more consistent-looking text.

Trade names take upper case: *Hoover* but *vacuum cleaner*, *Xerox* but *photocopier*, *Penbritin* but *ampicillin*.

The names of wars and historical periods normally take an initial capital: *Iron Age fort*, *Vietnam War*.

Acronyms usually take all capitals: BBC, EU, USA, TUC, FBI. Oxford's preferred style for acronyms that can be spoken as words is also all capitals: NATO, UNICEF and UNESCO. Most newspapers use Nato, Unicef and Unesco.

Hyphen (-)

Hyphens make links. For example, they link words that form a composite adjective before a noun: *computer-based work*, *short-term goals*, *half-inch nail*, *three-year-old child*, *out-of-hours work*, *no-go area* and *couldn't-care-less attitude*. This kind of hyphenation helps to reduce ambiguities and stumbles. A guest house says:

The new owners of this beautiful mansion take pride in their home cooked meals.

When the readers reach *home*, they may stop momentarily and think 'that's the end of the phrase', only to be caught out by the next word; *home-cooked* needs a hyphen.

The presence or absence of a hyphen can easily change the meaning. Compare:

The pop group reformed to The pop group re-formed.

The atrium has no smoking areas to The atrium has no-smoking areas.

A cross party spokesman to A cross-party spokesman.

The partnership seems to need extra marital sex to The partnership seems to need extra-marital sex.

There are no good lawyers in that firm to There are no-good lawyers in that firm.

Though their logic is clear enough, it is sometimes hard to justify hyphens that hang in a permanent state of separation from their companion, as in this sentence by Mary Killen in *The Times*:

A typical day's intake for me would include oat bran porridge for breakfast, flavoured with maple syrup, five wheat-, yeast- and sugar-free oatcakes mid-morning, baked potato, olive oil and salad for lunch, and hot vegetable stock at intervals until evening.

Consider this extract from a business proposal:

Normally on oil and gas related enquiries, a briefing meeting is convened at the client's request.

Gas related comes before *enquiries* and is effectively one word, so it needs a hyphen. But there are oil-related enquiries too in the sentence, because *related* is implied after *oil*. So the sentence should say, with a hyphen hanging after *oil*:

Normally on oil- and gas-related enquiries, a briefing meeting is convened at the client's request

or

Normally on oil-related and gas-related enquiries, a briefing meeting is convened at the client's request.

It is difficult to use hyphens consistently, and there is usually someone to disagree with your best efforts. The treasurer of the World Pheasant Association might be peering over your shoulder:

[Your] article . . . refers to the endangered 'white-eared pheasant' . . . The hyphen is incorrect. The pheasant in question is a white pheasant with ears. There are also blue eared pheasants and brown eared pheasants. The taxonomic similarity is that all the three pheasants have ears and all the ears are white.

When a woman was assaulted by a London taxi driver a newspaper described the attacker as a *black cab driver*. But which was black, the driver or the cab? The paper had meant to say *black-cab driver*, leaving his skin colour out of the question. Had it really wanted to mention his colour, it could have written *black black-cab driver* or *white black-cab driver*, but perhaps then it would have decided to recast the sentence.

It's normally unnecessary to hyphenate when one of the words is an adverb (see chapter 13):

rapidly growing economy; carefully crafted answer

though some newspapers routinely do this.

When nouns or adjectives, words with 'self' should be hyphenated: *self-esteem, self-employed, self-contained, self-centred, self-explanatory*. As *non-* is a hyphenated prefix, its hyphen is always present: *non-partisan, non-violent, non-qualifying, non-capital offering, non-aggression pact, non-aligned countries*. When attached to another adjective, *mid* always takes a hyphen: *mid-Victorian pottery, mid-ocean ridge, mid-engined vehicle*. A good dictionary will show which words are inherently hyphenated.

Some nouns formed by two or more words need hyphens: *set-up*, *set-to*, *run-up*, *build-up*, *free-for-all*, *call-out*, *punch-up*. Without a hyphen, there is ambiguity in sentences like:

Last week there was a bust up in the street

where the possible meanings include fight, drug bust or a piece of sculpture.

Verbs rarely need hyphenation – all three hyphens in this advertising leaflet are unnecessary, while a hyphen should have been included in *high-street bargains*:

With inflation decreasing, the press and politicians are spelling-out the message that the recession is over . . . Now is the time to think about making cash available for the numerous high street bargains and to begin paying-off some of the commitments that have built-up in this tough period.

In those cases, *spelling out*, *paying off* and *built up* were simply phrasal verbs (a verb followed by a particle). Verbs that do need hyphenating are usually compounds and are shown hyphenated in the dictionary, like to *fine-tune* a car, to *fine-draw* two pieces of cloth, to *double-check* an answer or to *copy-edit* some text.

Apostrophe (')

The apostrophe is now so widely misused – an errant tadpole, one columnist calls it – that its eventual death seems inevitable. Alongside their no-smoking stickers, companies could soon be declaring themselves apostrophe-free zones. This would be a pity, as the correct use of apostrophes conveys meaning and prevents ambiguity, while misplaced apostrophes make the reader stumble and backtrack.

The main rules on apostrophes are very simple and cover more than 99 per cent of cases. The few exceptions are more difficult and have to be memorized. The main rules deal with two matters, *possession* and *contraction*.

Possession

Follow a two-stage approach:

- First, find the possessor(s).
- Second, put an apostrophe immediately after the possessor(s).

For example, in:

The judges wig was eaten by the generals horse

it is clear that the judge possesses the wig and the general the horse, so the sentence becomes:

The judge's wig was eaten by the general's horse.

In:

The peoples leader ignored the childrens opinions

it is clear that the people possess the leader and the children the opinions, so the sentence – note carefully the position of the apostrophes – becomes:

The people's leader ignored the children's opinions.

The same rule applies to such sentences as:

The three inspectors' cars were attacked.

Several players' houses were daubed with paint

where the apostrophe goes immediately after the possessors.

It's a little more complicated when the singular form of a word ends in *s*, but you either add *'s* or just an apostrophe. Both these forms are correct:

I sent you Mr Jones's copy of the lease yesterday.

I sent you Mr Jones' copy of the lease yesterday.

Words that end in *ss* or *x*, like *boss*, *business* or *fox*, also take *'s* in possession:

The boss's failure to act led to orders being lost.

This surreal, apostrophe-free message is to be seen roaming Britain on a fleet of lorries:

COLLECTING TOMORROWS

DELIVERIES TODAY

As the deliveries belong to tomorrow, there should be an apostrophe between the *W* and *S*.

Contractions

Use an apostrophe to show that at least one letter is missing:

Today's the day for a fresh start (Today is . . .)

It's no concern of mine (It is . . .)

Doesn't anybody have the results? (Does not . . .)

Remember that pronouns – words in place of nouns – like *his*, *hers*, *ours*, *yours*, *theirs* and *its* don't need apostrophes. They are words in their own right – no letters are missing and the possession is built into the word. (The only exception is *one's*, as in *one's head is aching*.) So it would be correct to write:

The cat wandered in, its wet paws patterning the carpet.

Though the wet paws belong to the cat, there is no apostrophe in *its* because the possession is built into the word. Only insert an apostrophe in *its* when the word is short for *it is*.

In some expressions of measurement and time, apostrophes are conventional:

They took a week's holiday without permission and the firm then gave them two weeks' notice.

It is difficult to see the logic in this usage, but in the first example *holiday* in a sense belongs to the *week*. Without the apostrophe it would say:

a weeks holiday

which would mix a singular *a* with a plural-looking *weeks*. So, if it's logical to write a *week's holiday*, you should move the apostrophe along one letter when the possessor ends in *s*, as in *two weeks' notice*. This, however, is becoming extinct, whatever the logic.

Generally, don't use an apostrophe in a plural:

In the 1990s, people made more, spent more and saved less

unless there is possession:

Six MPs' offices were ransacked.

Refuse to be led astray by any shop notice proclaiming:

Shrimp's, prawns', pears', orange's and sandwich'es.

These are all straightforward plurals – no apostrophe is needed. Sometimes an exception to the rule is demanded by the need to avoid ambiguity. Hence:

Mind your p's and q's

A list of do's and don'ts

The first animal in the dictionary has three a's in its name

are preferable to:

Mind your ps and qs

A list of dos and don'ts

The first animal in the dictionary has three as in its name.

Occasionally you meet a rarity where at first the apostrophe looks superfluous:

Maria's lasagne was better than the chef's.

Clearly the lasagne belongs to Maria, so the first apostrophe is fine. But what belongs to the chef to deserve an apostrophe? Lasagne, again, because that word is implied. Had there been more than one chef, the apostrophe would have followed the *s*. The same thing happens with some shop names. *Lewis's*, in Liverpool, England means the shop belonging to Lewis.

In some cases, an apostrophe might seem appropriate but is unnecessary. If you call your office guidance on word processing a *Typists Handbook*, you could argue that it's a handbook *for* typists not *belonging* to them, so an apostrophe is not needed. The same could be true of Cashiers Office, and may explain why the National Association of Citizens Advice Bureaux has no apostrophe in its name – the bureaux do not *belong* to citizens, they are *for* citizens to use.

A final point: many keyboards hide true apostrophes and curly quotation marks but seductively offer instant access to the marks for feet (') and inches ("). Seek out the proper marks – they'll usually be hidden under another key.

Ellipsis (. . .)

The ellipsis has two purposes:

1   To show that material is missing, perhaps from a quotation. It is customary to put square brackets around this ellipsis, to avoid confusion with the second use of the ellipsis.

2   To indicate suspense:

He said: 'And the winner is . . . Sydney, Australia!'

There should be three dots in the ellipsis, not two, five or seven though a book reviewer tells me that when a phrase trails off unfinished, the US practice is to use four dots.

In typesetting or desk-top publishing, there is often a word space before and after each one, so . . . not... Some typesetters insist on adding a fourth dot when a sentence ends with an ellipsis, the fourth dot being set tight on the third to show its different character. Others are quite sure that the dots in the ellipsis should *not* have word spaces between them, but a word space before the first dot and after the last. Controversy rages, and consistency is hard to achieve.

Quotation marks (' ')

These, also called quotes, speech marks or inverted commas, indicate the opening and closing of direct speech:

'There is no alternative,' said the prime minister, 'so we will go on as before.'

Or, if the sentence ended after the first statement:

'There is no alternative,' said the prime minister. 'We will just go on and on as before.'

Note that in both cases the first comma comes within the closing quote in British English, as does the full stop after *before*.

Most books and newspapers use single quotes, reserving double quotes for a quotation within a quotation. The reverse is acceptable, though, and widespread in children's books and the US.

Quotes are also used to clothe a word in irony or, usually unnecessarily, to apologize for some clumsy or supposedly colloquial usage:

Recently I have been 'toying' with the idea of buying a mobile phone and wondered if you were going to sell them.

In this preliminary phase I also 'touched base' with many other interested people.

Quotes are common when drawing attention to the first use of a technical term:

This kind of score is known as the 'median'.

In British English, when quoting a full sentence from another source, put your closing full stop inside the closing quotes:

We agree with the president when he says, 'New Coke is best.'

When quoting a sentence fragment, the closing full stop goes outside the closing quote:

He told us to 'get a life' and 'pay less attention to punctuation and more to growing the business'.

Just to confuse things, in US English that final quote mark would go outside the full stop (period), and the quote marks would usually be double. Moreover, in quoted sentence fragments that need to be followed by a comma, the comma will come inside the quote marks in a formation that looks as bizarre to British eyes as the opposite must look to Americans:

Naturally the telemarketeer must be prepared for all possible answers like 'in the morning,' 'on weekends,' 'after midnight,' or 'between 3 a.m. and 4 a.m.' (Gary Blake, *Quick Tips for Better Business Writing*, New York 1995)

Exclamation mark (!)

Use this to follow exclamations of surprise, shock or dismay, but sparingly and singly!!! Using the mark to signal a witticism or acute observation not only deprives readers of the pleasure of noticing it for themselves, but suggests they are too slow to see it without help.

Question mark (?)

Use this after direct questions. There is no need for one if the question is really a polite demand:

Will you please let me have your reply by 6pm today.

In informal writing, a bracketed question mark is useful for drawing attention to a doubtful claim:

His department is addicted to cutting-edge (?) technology.

12 | Seven writing myths explored and exploded

Guideline: *Avoid being enslaved by writing myths.*

A business writer once told me she had been instructed by her English teacher never to begin consecutive paragraphs with the same letter of the alphabet. After 30 years of following this non-rule, she said she was beginning to wonder if there was any justification for it.

Your path as a writer is steep enough without the extra burden of schoolroom mythology. This chapter examines some of the most tenacious non-rules imposed on writers.

Myth 1: You must not start a sentence with 'but'

By some people, this ban is even extended to 'so', 'because', 'and' and 'however'. But it is not a rule of grammar or even a widely observed convention, and may stem from a desire among teachers to persuade children to link up the sentence fragments they tend to write.

Most influential authors in the last few hundred years have ignored the myth. In *A Vindication of the Rights of Woman* (1792) Mary Wollstonecraft regularly uses 'but' and 'and' to begin sentences. Jane Austen starts hers with 'but' on almost every page of her novels, and occasionally uses 'and' in the same position, in the sense of 'furthermore'. This is one of her buts from *Mansfield Park* (1814), where it stops the bland first sentence running on too long and heightens its contrast with the ironic second:

> She had two sisters to be benefited by her elevation [marriage to a social superior]; and such of their acquaintance as thought Miss Ward and Miss Frances quite as handsome as Miss Maria, did not scruple to predict their marrying with almost equal advantage. But there certainly are not so many men of large fortune in the world, as there are pretty women to deserve them.

'But', like most sentence connectors, signals a shift in pace and direction. It may help in stating an argument or point of view, as in this example from a modern British journalist who, for emphasis, happily begins the final sentence with 'And':

The children of MPs, royalty, journalists and other moral prodnoses do not need to read underclass horror-stories to find out about the lifestyle problems which adult sexuality inflicts on children. They are familiar with it all: access arrangements, vendettas, embarrassment, lawsuits, confusion, hypocrisy. 'I believe strenuously,' says Mrs Nicholson [a British MP], 'that every child deserves a mother and father'; and so say all of us. But the plain fact is that not every child has them to hand. And in family life, the golden rule is to start from where you are.

Even old-time grammarians felt able to start sentences with 'but'. In his *Manual of English Grammar and Composition* (1915), J C Nesfield says:

. . . it is convenient for the sake of brevity to say that 'a conjunction joins words to words, and sentences to sentences'. But this is not enough for the purposes of definition.

People sometimes say that starting with 'but' is unbusinesslike. But what's so special about business writing that the norm in every other kind of writing is to be set aside?

'So' is a useful alternative to 'consequently', 'therefore' and 'as a result' at the start of a sentence, especially if you are a slow typist:

So it would seem that the courts may override the words which the parties have used, in the process of interpreting a written contract, despite the powerful authorities which I have mentioned.
(Sir Christopher Staughton, former Lord Justice of Appeal, England and Wales, writing in *Clarity* 50, pp 24–29)

When so many obviously careful writers show by their own practices that they disregard the myth, the best advice is that you may start a sentence with any word you want, so long as the sentence hangs together as a complete statement. Even to begin a sentence with 'and', in the sense of 'furthermore', is fairly common among journalists and novelists who want its extra dramatic effect. Here, Philip Howard of *The Times*, writing in 2004 about the altered meanings of military metaphors like 'putting yourself in the firing line', uses 'And so' (meaning 'Thus') to begin a sentence:

> The first citation of the phrase comes from our defeat by the Boers at Majuba in 1881. 'General Stewart was obliged to put every reserve man into the firing line.' As rifles became more accurate, it was no longer necessary or tactically sensible to concentrate your rifles into a firing line. And so our firing line has changed from attackers to targets.

The device is not new, even in prose that purples at the edges. Reporting the Coronation in 1953, *The Times* wrote:

> And already waiting for her, on every stretch of her way to and from the Abbey, is the homage of which flag and symbol and flower are no more than an expression – the love and loyal service of her people.

Myth 2: You must not put a comma before 'and'

Many folk insist that putting a comma before 'and' is bad. Ignore them. (Just as Nesfield did, in the second line of the earlier example.) Though a comma is usually unnecessary in this position, it may help the reader to see how the sentence is constructed, or put a pause exactly where you want it. A few examples:

> It was a bright cold day in April, and the clocks were striking thirteen. (First line of Orwell's *Nineteen Eighty-four*)

> Parents shop around. They send for a clutch of prospectuses, see what's available in both the public and private sectors, and are prepared to switch their children between the two at different stages in their education. (*The Times*, 1994)

> When we met last night, you explained that you no longer wished me to remain as Secretary of State for Education, and I am writing to say how glad I have been to serve in Her Majesty's Government. (Letter of resignation to the British prime minister, 1994)

And here is Beatrix Potter, setting an example to children in *The Tale of Peter Rabbit*:

> He found a door in a wall; but it was locked, and there was no room for a fat little rabbit to squeeze underneath.

Myth 3: You must not end a sentence with a preposition

A few fossils believe that a sentence is bad if it ends in a preposition. According to them, these are ungrammatical:

There are certain values we must all be prepared to stand up for.

... the thousand natural shocks that flesh is heir to. (Shakespeare)

The council decided this was the right system to invest in.

You do not have to complete this section if you prefer not to.

What are you talking about?

It's true that the first could be recast as:

There are certain values for which we must all be prepared to stand up

but this would still annoy anyone who thinks 'up' is a preposition here (actually it's a particle attached to the verb). There is no point changing a sentence that reads well, sounds right and says what the writer wants to say, just because it contravenes the myth. Sometimes sentences ending in prepositions do need to be recast, but this is because they read awkwardly, not because they break a rule. These sentences, for example, come to a feeble end:

Get clean photocopies of the forms you want to make changes to.
Make sure there is enough white space to mark your alterations on.

Better to write:

Get clean photocopies of the forms you want to change. Make sure there is enough white space for marking your alterations.

Myth 4: You must not split your infinitives

Splitting the infinitive means putting a word or phrase between 'to' and the verb word, as in:

The department wants to <u>more than</u> double its budget.

The passengers were asked to <u>carefully</u> get down from the train.

If you think a sentence will be more emphatic, clear or rhythmical, split your infinitive – there is no reason in logic or grammar for avoiding it. The examples above seem better split than not. Take care, though, lest the gap between 'to' and the verb word becomes too great, as the reader could lose track of the meaning.

A newspaper editorial says:

The most diligent search can find no modern grammarian to pedantically, to dogmatically, to invariably condemn a split infinitive. Rules are created to aid the communication of meaning. In the cause of meaning they can sometimes be broken.

Though this is excellent, it encourages the idea that to split an infinitive is to break a rule. Yet there is no such rule, merely a superstition that arose in the nineteenth century when grammarians sought to impose Latin rules on English. In Latin, a present-tense infinitive is always a single, unsplittable word: *amare*, *cantare*, *audire*.

If you can't bring yourself to split an infinitive, at least allow others the freedom to do so. For example, Byron, with his:

To slowly trace the forest's shady scene.

Phrases like 'I easily won the race' and 'he quickly drove away' are not split infinitives as there is no infinitive present.

Myth 5: You must not write a one-sentence paragraph

If you can say what you want to say in a single sentence that lacks a direct connection with any other sentence, just stop there and go on to a new paragraph; there's no rule against it. A paragraph can be a single sentence, whether long, short or middling.

Myth 6: You should write as you speak

This advice is widely heard, but take it with a large pinch of salt. True, many writers would benefit from making their writing more conversational, using more personal pronouns and active verbs. But this is not the same as writing as you speak. Most of us don't speak in complete sentences – a transcript of our talk usually reads like gibberish on the page. Good, clear writing is much more than speech transcribed; it is speech organized, worked and refined.

Myth 7: You should test your writing with a readability formula

Several software grammar-checkers (such as Microsoft Word's inbuilt program, and StyleWriter) claim to measure the readability of writing under such names as the FOG (frequency of gobbledygook) Index and the Flesch Test. Generally these tests or formulas use only two variables to get their results: sentence length and vocabulary load (such as word length or rarity). The score is then compared to a reading age level (UK), grade level (US) or the level of some typical texts, and a comparison is produced. The formulas cannot take into account the way the information is organized, how it looks on the page, and the reader's motivation and level of prior knowledge. They give only the merest hint about how to write a text better, and they encourage the idea that a clear document is one that scores well on a formula. So they are fairly blunt analytical tools.

If you lack the software to perform a readability test, here is a method based on that devised by Robert Gunning:

1 Count a passage of text roughly 300 words long, ending with a full stop. Number of words = A.

2 Work out the average sentence length, B.

3 Count the number of words of three or more syllables, excluding those that start with capitals, or have three or more syllables only because they have had -ing, -ed or -es added, or combine two short words such as 'pro-choice' or 'photofit'. This gives you the number of 'hard words'. Multiply it by $100/A$, to give C.

4 Then add B to C and multiply by 0.4.

5 This gives the lowest US grade level that could easily read the text, so add 5 to give the British reading age. It's worth remembering that beyond about 12th grade (British reading age 17), grades and reading ages become pretty meaningless.

The formulas do have one useful purpose: to act as a yardstick. Say a firm does consultancy work for its customers and writes reports for them. It can decide that the reports must score below a certain level on the formula, otherwise they will not be published without further editing. The yardstick acts as a constant reminder to authors, who can then be encouraged to attend writing-skills courses and consider guidelines such as those in this book.

Except for that purpose, the formulas are very limited. It is true that they are better than nothing, but careful analysis of a text and testing with users are likely to produce more meaningful results.

13 | Conquering grammarphobia

Guideline: *You can be a good writer without learning hundreds of grammatical terms.*

Grammarphobia – an irrational terror of grammatical terminology – is common among those who underwent grammar lessons at school and those who did not. The first group might regard grammar as just one more abstract ritual to be endured while the sun shone outside; the second group might see it as a magical key to successful writing, unreasonably withheld from them by malevolent educationists – especially, in the UK, from 1960–90.

A little grammar goes a long way. It is not necessary to know much beyond well-taught primary-school grammar in order to write plain English, but it's helpful to know a few terms if only to get the most out of books in this field. This chapter provides a brief glossary of the grammatical terms in most common use. When reading it, remember that many words change their grammatical character depending on their role in a sentence. Just because 'progress' is a noun in this sentence:

We will make progress on the project next week

doesn't stop it becoming a verb in this one:

I have progressed further than expected.

Adjective A word of description. In 'local residents have demanded safer streets', 'local' and 'safer' are adjectives describing their respective nouns.

Adverb Most adverbs end in *-ly* such as *certainly*, *quickly*, *sadly*, *probably*, but non *-ly* forms include *often*, *soon*, *away*. There are two types. First, verb-phrase adverbs that say how the action in the verb takes place, such as the words underlined here:

The politician <u>quietly</u> but <u>firmly</u> argued for more investment in the railways.

Second, sentence adverbs that show the speaker's attitude to what's being said:

**Understandably, the miners demanded better pay and conditions.
The coal-owners, not surprisingly, refused.**

Clause A group of words, often not a complete sentence, containing such things as a doer and verb. There are two clauses in: 'If there were no bad people, there would be no good lawyers.'

Contraction A word with one or more letters missing and replaced by an apostrophe, for example: *don't* (do not), *won't* (will not), *haven't* (have not), *can't* (cannot), *I'd* (I would or I should). In informal and semi-formal business writing, contractions can add a little conversational warmth. The more unusual ones, like *you'll* (you will), *there'll* (there will), *there're* (there are) and *you'd* (you would) look odd in formal letters and reports, but if you use them make sure the apostrophes go in the right places.

Co-ordinator A word that links two or more words, sentences or clauses, for example: *but, when, and, yet, if, although.*

Doer The person doing the action in a sentence, also known as the agent. In 'The publisher sent the contract', 'publisher' is the doer.

Grammar The body of rules and conventions by which words are grouped in a way that is meaningful to other people. For example, the sentence 'Paris look a beautiful city' is ungrammatical – if standard English is the criterion – as it breaks the rule that a singular doer must govern a singular form of the verb. Non-standard English uses different grammar which can be just as effective in the right circumstances. Bob Marley, the reggae musician (died 1981), sang of his ancestors: 'Pirates, yes they rob I / Sold I to the merchant ships / Minutes after they took I / From the bottomless pit.' Usage changes over time: Queen Victoria of the United Kingdom (died 1901) was quite happy to write 'The news from France are very bad' because in her day 'news' was an accepted plural. It also changes from place to place: in British sports commentary, national and local teams tend to be plural – 'England are winning 2–0' – while in Australian commentary, teams are usually singular.

Imperative The form of the verb that gives commands, for example: *go, eat, push, don't jump, let them go, let me see, don't be deceived.*

Infinitive The basic form of the verb, made up of *to* plus the verb word. Present-tense infinitives include *to go, to eat, to dream.* Past-tense infinitives include *to have gone, to have eaten, to have dreamt.* Passive-voice infinitives include *to be eaten, to be attacked.*

Nominalization A noun phrase formed from a verb, for example *preparation* (from *to prepare*), *renewal* (from *to renew*).

Noun A word that signifies a person, thing, place, activity or quality, for example *axe, beacon, carrot, dam, eating, frill, gerbil, happiness.* Proper nouns are specific names of people, places and the like: *Christmas, Canberra, Canada, Caroline.*

Object The thing to which some action is done: 'we destroyed the *ship.*'

Paragraph A sentence or group of sentences separated in some way from the rest of the text and dealing with a particular part of the topic being discussed.

Participle The present participle adds *-ing* to the verb, hence *going, finding, sleeping.* The past participle adds *-d* or *-ed* to most verbs, as in *worked, decided, starved.* See chapter 4 for the way other past participles are formed.

Particle Many words that act as prepositions can also be adverb particles. In 'The relationship was broken off' and 'My car has broken down', the words 'off' and 'down' are particles. You can tell this because they lack objects.

Plural More than one. 'Frogs' is the plural of 'frog', which is singular. Where optional plurals are available for words of Latin or Greek origin, favour the English. Hence *referendums* not *referenda, forums* not *fora, stadiums* not *stadia, formulas* not *formulae.* But *criteria* not *criterions, phenomena* not *phenomenons.*

Preposition A word that usually comes immediately before a noun or pronoun, such as *in, down, up, under, of, with, by, to, from, at*: 'my car rolled *down* the hill and *under* the bridge.' Prepositions have objects, 'hill' and 'bridge' being the objects in that sentence. See Particle.

Pronoun A word that stands in place of nouns, for example *he*, *she*, *it*, *him*, *you*, *I*, *me*, *they*, *anyone*.

Sentence A statement, question, exclamation or command – usually starting with a capital letter and ending in a full stop – which is complete in itself as the expression of a thought. Grammarians differ on what constitutes a sentence, but it is easiest to think of it as a finished utterance that makes sense in its context. Thus it will usually have a finite (finished) verb. These, for example, are sentences:

My business will succeed, no matter what.

Having succeeded in its first two years, my business will keep growing.

Referring to your letter of 21 January, I can see no cause for alarm.

But these are not sentences:

My business will succeed, no matter what anyone.

Having succeeded in its first two years.

Referring to your letter of 21 January.

Examples like the following can be classed as sentences even though they lack verbs, provided they make sense in context. The verbs are implied and shown here in square brackets:

[This is] Not so.

[That would happen] Over my dead body.

[This has been] A great success for all concerned.

Singular See Plural.

Subject The noun or pronoun that agrees with the verb. In 'My elephant needs water' and 'The postilion has been struck by lightning', the words 'elephant' and 'postilion' are the subjects.

Tense This refers to when an action occurs:

- Present tenses: *he goes*; *he is going*; *she survives*; *she is surviving*.
- Conditional: *she would go*; *they would see*.
- Future tense: *he will go*; *she will survive*.
- Past tenses: *he went*; *he has gone*; *he had gone*; *she survived*; *she has survived*; *she had survived*.

Verb Verbs express an action (*eat, sleep*) or a mental state (*know, believe*), so they are often described as doing words. A more accurate description is time-action words because the action takes place in past, present or future time. In active-voice verbs, the doer normally comes in front of the verb: *Goats destroy vegetation*; *Pigs might fly*. In passive-voice verbs, the doer normally comes after the verb: *Vegetation is destroyed by goats*, or is not present at all. See chapter 4 for more on this.

14 | Planning effectively

Guideline: *Plan before you write.*

'I don't know how to get started' is a common complaint. In the 'weaknesses' section of her pre-attendance form, one of my writing-course students declared: 'Before I start I often have to think for some time about what I am going to write.'

Thinking before writing is usually a strength, and many people find that the best way to start writing (or dictating) is not to write but to plan. The first stage of planning is to think out:

- who is going to read the document;
- what they will be expecting to get from it;
- in what circumstances they will be reading (in their leisure time; at work in a quarry or on a building site; on a website; underwater);
- what you're trying to achieve.

It is better to plan on paper or on a computer screen than in your head. This is because most people's brains are better at marshalling ideas when they are set down on the page. It's difficult to hold 20 points in your head while simultaneously assessing them for strength and relevance and grouping them into bundles of related points. For one thing, you're having to assess which of the two million billion possible ways of ranking the points is the best.

For a short document, keep the plan simple. Make a list or bubble diagram containing all the points you expect to make, *in no particular order*. (Overleaf is a bubble diagram of my first thoughts for writing chapter 21.) Cross out the irrelevant points. Link the rest into groups of related points. Rank them using one of the structures in chapter 15. Then you will have a good framework from which to write or dictate. Don't skimp this stage, but don't overdo it to the point of boredom.

Longer documents benefit from fuller planning. If your managers ask you to write a report, discuss exactly what's wanted so that you are clear on the purpose and the amount of detail expected – otherwise you'll waste time on soul-destroying rewrites. If your managers don't really know what they want, you should investigate the topic thoroughly and return with a core statement (explained next) which sets out the purpose of the document as you see it.

Creating a core statement and horizontal document plan

A core statement says what you will cover in the main section of the document – normally the discussion section. It helps you to focus on the task and the audience. Sharpening your focus in this way will save you researching topics that don't need to be covered. The core statement also builds your confidence as it provides your first glimpse of the finishing line.

The core statement is a rigidly constructed sentence in seven segments, as shown next. The oblique strokes separate alternative words and phrases that you might use:

Core segments	Typical phrases
1 Type of document	This report/paper
2 Your readers	to the head of the legal department
3 Verb	describes/assesses/explains/analyses/ evaluates/considers/investigates
4 Topic	possible improvements to the clarity of our insurance policies
5 Linking phrase	in terms of/with reference to/under
6 Number of sections	six main lines of enquiry
7 Main headings	– benefits and dangers
	– what documents will be worked on?
	– implications for staff training
	– other companies' experience
	– legal requirements
	– costs

Don't expect to write the core statement in ten seconds. You may need several attempts at choosing the best verb in segment 3. Discuss the core statement with your manager, agree any changes and get him or her to sign it off. This reduces the chance of creating a report nobody wants.

The core statement underlies the next stage of planning – the horizontal document plan. Regard this as a series of related boxes into which you slot all the points you expect to make under the headings set by the core statement. The main practical points are:

- Use the biggest sheet of paper around (prefer A3 to A4).
- Rotate the page so that the longer edge is nearer to you (landscape).
- Set down your headings along the top.
- Jot down all the points you can think of under that heading. Usually you will want to create a system of sub-headings within each section: boxes nested within boxes.

Let's assume the core statement said:

This report to the head of the legal department describes possible improvements to the clarity of our insurance policies under six main

lines of enquiry: benefits and dangers; what documents will be
worked on; implications for staff training; other companies'
experience; legal requirements; costs.

A much-simplified (and tidied up) horizontal document plan for
two sections of the report might look like this:

Benefits and Dangers	Complications for staff training
Benefits	Direct sales staff
• Focus for an advertising + sales campaign	• No new training required – in effect same policies.
• Get in line with marketplace – customer satisfaction	• Explain purpose and discuss likely customer responses.
• Clear English Standard	• New selling points (clear, simple, easy to use).
• Compliance with EU directive	
Dangers	**Head office staff**
• Legal safety – consult lawyers/ counsel	• Briefing on new features for all in direct customer contact.
• Confusion among existing customers?	• Explain philosophy.

You can then assess the points for strength and relevance and, if
necessary, group them under further sub-headings. Gaps in your
knowledge may be revealed; you may need to fill them before pro-
ceeding. Next, put the headings and points in order, perhaps using
one of the structures in chapter 15. Show a tidy version of the plan
to your manager. Discuss it with him or her. Get it signed off.

The writing itself can now begin. As you write you will probably
change your mind about the order of points, and add to the plan.
This is fine – the plan is meant to be a working document. One tip
when you do start to write: there is no need to begin at the beginning. Provided they are self-contained, the bits you are confident
about and know best can be written first. Then you will be less anxious about tackling the rest.

I have assumed that you are the sole writer on this project. If you
are part of a team, the core statement and horizontal document

plan can be prepared collaboratively, using a white board or similar. Then all the team members can take part in creating a common purpose and plan for the report, and will write individual sections with a better awareness of how their part fits in to the whole.

Alternative approaches to planning

Writers I have worked with seem to perform better when they plan. They also *believe* they write better and more quickly. But not everyone is happy to plan to the same extent: there are differing approaches, all with their followers. For convenience, four main labels can be used to represent these approaches: 'architects', 'watercolourists', 'oil painters' and 'bricklayers'. You may like to consider which category you fit into and whether the alternatives might suit you better. Bear in mind, though, that most writers fit into two or more of the categories from time to time.

- **Architects** tend to take a three-stage approach to writing: planning, writing and revising. They do not try to perfect the writing as they create the first draft. They prefer to leave a draft and come back to it later, revising thoroughly on paper or on screen.
- **Watercolourists** try to produce a complete version rapidly at the first attempt, with little revision. There may have been little planning on paper but long mental incubation of the document. Some literary writers are said to favour this, believing that it keeps their writing spontaneous and true to feeling.
- **Oil painters** tend to jot down ideas and then organize and repeatedly rework them. On paper there is little planning. Rewriting seems to help oil painters to find out what they think, rather than helping them to focus on the readers' needs.
- **Bricklayers** tend to polish every sentence before going on to the next, in a careful process of building block by block. This means they revise very little once a first draft has been prepared. Bricklayers tend to plan and have a clear idea of what they want to say from the outset. They tend not to regard writing as an aid to thinking.

Given the importance of careful thought about the readers' needs when preparing plain-English documents, the architectural approach, with its bias towards planning, seems to be the most suitable. Again, though, you should be ready to experiment, use different strategies for different tasks, and do whatever will get the writing job completed to a satisfactory standard with the minimum of effort.

If you can't see yourself in any of the above categories, here is another way of looking at it, based on the ideas of Dr Betty S Flowers. Her paradigm (or writing model) separates writing into four stages, each requiring the writer to take a different approach and assume four different personalities. They are described thus by the Australian plain-language practitioner, Christopher Balmford:

- **The madman** who brainstorms, takes notes, and is enthusiastic, experimental and above all creative.
- **The architect** who reviews the information that the madman has created and gathered, and uses it to develop an outline of the document.
- **The carpenter** who fleshes out the structure by writing the text and producing the first [or] (however many) drafts.
- **The judge** who edits and reviews [the] drafts.

All the personalities are vital to the writing process, but the architect has the key job of dividing, classifying and sequencing the information.

Strategic planning: learning from readers

A strategic plan may be necessary, especially when preparing a major document for internal or public use. The plan below relates to the preparation of a booklet for staff joining a company pension scheme, but many of its points are universal. The plan builds in plenty of reader involvement – essential unless secrecy, deadlines or costs prevent it.

Pre-production stage

- Decide purpose. Why is the booklet needed? Would something else do a better job?
- Determine the content. At this stage, just outline main points.
- Define the audience. Consult staff to see what they expect from the booklet. Discuss the outline. If possible, get an idea of how they would like the information organized and even what they'd like it to say.
- Consider how the booklet fits into the system. How will it be distributed, used, stored? Will it be downloadable from your company website? How will it be amended in future? What organizational politics will need to be dealt with and how?

Production stage

- Fill in the outline of the content. Decide what structure is most suitable.
- Write the draft. Include headings and sub-headings but don't worry about adding too many layout features at this stage.
- Evaluate the draft with staff – include some who haven't yet been consulted. Use a questionnaire to test comprehension. Iron out problems by redrafting and restructuring.
- Prepare an appropriate layout. Use professional help if necessary. Evaluate the layout with staff.

Post-production stage

- Final evaluation: after distribution, use a survey and face-to-face discussions to gauge reactions. Did the booklet do its job?
- Keep it up to date by regular reviews.

15 | Using reader-centred structure

Guideline: *Organize your material in a way that helps readers to grasp the important information early and to navigate through the document easily.*

You might be lucky. Your readers might regard your letter or report as the highlight of their day. They might give it the time you know it deserves. They might sit back in a comfy armchair and browse through it contentedly for hours.

Or you might be like most other writers. Your document will be an interruption to your readers' busy day. They'll read it in haste, scribbling remarks on it and picking out important bits with a high-lighter pen. And they'll be asking two questions with every sentence they read:

- So what?
- How does this affect me?

Answering these questions in plain words and short sentences won't always be enough. You will also need to organize the material so that readers can extract what they want in the shortest possible time. This will increase the likelihood of getting your ideas read – the first step in getting them accepted. And a crucial way of organizing material well is to put important news early. Then readers can see, right from the start, exactly what you're getting at. This is particularly important on web pages, where limited screen space means that the top half of a page is more likely to be read.

This chapter shows ten ways ('models') of organizing your information. Don't feel that you have to force your writing to fit the models or, where headings are suggested, that you have to use the exact words. Quarry them for ideas that will suit your own way of doing things.

Model 1: Top-heavy triangle

Put your most important point first, follow it with the next most important, and so on, until your last paragraph includes relatively minor points. You may need to do a bit of scene-setting to start with – use the first sentence or the heading for this:

John

Scene-setting	**Request for leave from 25 March – 12 April** Thanks for your e-mail message yesterday.
Big news	The managing director has agreed to your request to take special unpaid leave immediately after your visit to Athens. It is vital, though, that we have a brief written report of your key findings as soon as the business part of the trip is completed. Will you please e-mail or fax this to us on 24 March.
Less important	As your flight was booked some time ago, please liaise with Michael South about rearranging the return leg.
Minor points	Hope this helps. We'll speak again after Tuesday's meeting.

Even unwelcome news should usually be delivered early. You may need to soften it, though:

John

	Request for leave from 25 March – 12 April
Scene-setting	Thanks for your e-mail message yesterday.
Big news	The managing director considered your request carefully but I'm sorry to tell you that he has had to say no. He feels that the launch of the new product at the end of March really demands your presence here.
Minor points	I realize you'll be disappointed but perhaps we can have a chat about things after next Tuesday's meeting.

I know of only one good reason for saving big news till the end – deliberate obfuscation, when delay will increase surprise, raise tension or leave the reader with a sense of threat.

The top-heavy triangle is useful when you're asking for something your readers may be reluctant to give. The letter below is trying to get local traders to fill in a questionnaire. But where does this vital information come?

Dear Mr Jones

Our Sea Fishery Group is conducting studies in order to aid the development of a local Fishery Forum. The idea of a Fishery Forum is to promote the fishing industry of the north west and to stress the importance of a regional approach as this could attract support from the European Union.

The study is designed to help evaluate the monetary impact that fish landings from the north west fishing fleet have on the region as a whole. Also the study will assess the feasibility of placing a logo on local fish products so that their origins can be instantly recognized.

To gather information for the study, a questionnaire has been designed. It is hoped that a high proportion of these forms will be completed and returned so that the final analysis will be as detailed as possible.

All answers to the questionnaires will be confidential and only the combined figures for the whole region would be published.

I would greatly appreciate it if you could complete the enclosed questionnaire by 15 June and return it to me. If you have any queries about the study or the questionnaire, please contact me on the above number. Thank you for your help.

The readers only learn the main action point in the final paragraph, and they might never get there. It would have been better to begin with an explanatory heading and the plea for help.

Dear Mr Jones

IMPROVING THE PROSPERITY OF THE NORTH WEST

I'm writing to ask for your help with a venture that will ultimately improve the prosperity of our region and of every trader who does business here.

Our Sea Fishery Group is conducting research into setting up a Fishery Forum that would promote our local fishing industry.

As part of the research, I need your help. Would you please be kind enough to complete the enclosed questionnaire and return it to me by 15 June? [etc]

In long letters or long e-mails that deal with several different issues, it's a good idea to use a heading for each issue. The heading can be placed between paragraphs or form the first few words of the paragraph, in bold or italic type. The top-heavy triangle can then be used when arranging the points in each headed section. When responding to long and rambling letters of complaint, ombudsmen and regulators often begin, 'From your letter, I understand that your main complaints are . . .', followed by a bullet list. This is good practice: it sets out what issues will be dealt with and enables the complainant to object if the issues have been wrongly summarized.

Model 2: Problem–Cause–Solution

This is a simple model for short letters, e-mails and reports. First you state the problem . . .

You asked me to find out how a batch of chocolate came to be contaminated during the night shift on 25 April.

Then you state the cause . . .

What seems to have happened is that some inadequately treated reclaimed chocolate was added to the mix. This occurred because the reclaimed chocolate was mis-labelled and stored in the wrong part of the factory.

Then you say what should happen in the future . . .

The contaminated batch will have to be destroyed. The cost of the loss is about £2,800, taking everything into account. I have told supervisors to tighten their procedures for labelling and storage. They'll be reporting back to me next week.

Model 3: Chronological order

This simply follows the time sequence of a series of actions or events, which can be paragraphed, numbered or dated depending on the purpose. For more on using chronological-order instructions, see chapter 19.

Model 4: Questions and answers

Questions and answers help to break up the information into small chunks. Here is an excellent example which also benefits from short paragraphs and everyday English:

How do I make a complaint about the council's services?

If you have a complaint, please take it up first with the department that deals with the subject of your complaint. Contact them and try to get the problem settled there and then. Phone numbers of departments are shown at the end of the leaflet.

What if I am not satisfied?

If you are not satisfied or your complaint is complicated, please set out all the facts clearly by making a formal complaint in writing. You can do this on the pull-out form opposite. If you need help to complete the form, please ask at any council office. We will acknowledge your complaint and keep you informed at every stage.

Where else can I get help?

If you are not satisfied with the way your complaint is dealt with, you could contact one of your ward councillors. A list is available at all of our reception desks and from Member Services. (Telephone: Cadeby 4000.)

Questions tend to provoke interest in readers by bringing them into the action. It is customary to reiterate at least part of the question when answering it. So the answer to 'What if I am not satisfied' begins 'If you are not satisfied . . .'. This may be tedious but seems to help the readers.

Questions are particularly useful if they use personal words. Compare:

Where can more information be obtained?

with

Where can I get more information?

Questions also convert dull, plodding label-headings into verb-rich information. Compare this heading:

Frequency of use by paramedics of aspirin in the treatment of heart-attack victims

with its equivalent question:

How often do paramedics use aspirin to treat heart-attack victims?

or, in the passive to put the stress on 'aspirin':

How often is aspirin used by paramedics to treat heart-attack
victims?

Model 5: S-C-R-A-P (Situation, Complication, Resolution, Action, Politeness)

A corny mnemonic, but useful. A letter or e-mail using this structure might say:

Dear Mr Soaring

**Order for 5 Sky-Fly hang gliders,
£2,250 each**

Situation	Thank you for your order dated 17 December; my apologies for the delay in responding.
Complication	The manufacturers have recently withdrawn the Sky-Fly and now offer a much-improved model, the Sky Jet. I enclose a leaflet which gives details of all its features.
Resolution	Although the price of the Sky Jet is £255 more than the old model, I can offer it to you at a special introductory price of £2,385 until 10 January next. We could let you have immediate delivery.
Action	If you would like to order the new model at the discount price, do please contact us. We accept payment by cheque and all major credit cards.
Politeness	I look forward to hearing from you.

Model 6: S-O-A-P (Situation, Objective, Appraisal, Proposal)

Here's a much-simplified short report that uses SOAP:

FALL IN SALES OF RABBIT CHOCOLATE BARS

Situation

In the last three months, Rabbit has lost about 10 per cent of its share
in the aphrodisiac chocolate bar market.

Objective

To regain and improve market share in the next six months.

Appraisal

The impact of our initial advertising and promotional burst has petered out. Research shows the recent price increase didn't affect sales very much but Rabbit has started losing ground to similar-priced competitors like the Hunky bar and the Rhino bar: people are seeing them as more sophisticated products.

Proposal

Target the higher social groups with a more sophisticated campaign based on Beatrix Potter stereotypes, including special-offer shooting weekends in Brer Rabbit country.

Model 7: PARbox e-mails and memos

Some firms, infuriated at the time-wasting woolliness of inter-office e-mails and memos, insist that all begin with three standard boxes for Purpose, Action and Response:

> **Purpose**
> To explain developments in The Savill fraud case

> **Action requested**
> Your help in unearthing missing documents

> **Response required**
> By 10 January

Readers can then immediately see the key facts and fit the request into their schedule.

After the PARboxes come a main heading and text as normal.

Model 8: The 5 P's
(Position, Problem, Possibilities,
Proposal, Packaging)

Using these headings, a short and very simplified report for a sports club might say:

UPDATE ON OUR LEAGUE PLACING

1   Position
1.1   With only 10 games to go this season, the team is close to the relegation zone.

1.2   The coach's contract has two years to run at £70K a year. He is widely respected in the town and throughout the sport.

2   Problem
2.1   Recent results have been very bad – 9 defeats and 2 draws in the last 11 games. Attendances are down 10 per cent on last season's and our overdraft stands at £3m. The fans are restless and some have started barracking the coach.

3   Possibilities
3.1   We could buy new players before the transfer deadline – the coach's proposals are attached.

3.2   We could terminate the coach's contract immediately but this would be costly and very unpopular with most of the fans. It could also damage team morale.

3.3   We could leave things as they are.

4   Proposal
4.1   We should try to buy Player A to improve the defence. Apart from that, we should leave things as they are because:
   (a) there's little cash for new players or buying out the coach's contract;
   (b) two key players will soon return from injury;
   (c) the team has played better recently and the last two defeats were very narrow.

5   Packaging
5.1   It may be a cliché, but we need to express full confidence in the players and the coach and say that they would benefit from the continued support of the fans. We need to explain the club's financial position better. We need to reassure supporters that their views will continue to be considered.

In the report I have added a commonly used system of paragraph numbering. The aim is to help readers to navigate through the report and, if necessary, comment on it more easily. An alternative to a decimal system is simply to number paragraphs in 1–2–3 order. In either system, if you use a second tier of heading, you don't need to number it but you should distinguish it by layout, perhaps with bold type or underlining.

Avoid creating a third or fourth level of decimals (3.1.2 etc) unless the amount of detail really demands it. Many readers will boggle at such complications.

Model 9: Correspondent's order

It's possible to respond to some letters or e-mails using the same order of points as your correspondent. Normally it's wise to say that this is what you're doing:

I'd like to respond to your points in the same order that you used.

Model 10: Full-dress report

A good arrangement for a detailed administrative or technical report or consultation paper is given below. Notice that the summary is placed early, though it will be written late in the process. A scientific report would also have sections for 'method' and 'results', which would follow the introduction, and perhaps an abstract (a kind of condensed summary that can be included in a database of abstracts along with a list of key words and phrases that researchers will look for as they trawl the database).

Title
The title says what the topic is, briefly but not too cryptically. If necessary, add a longer sub-title. Also add the author's name, the date and the distribution list.

Contents list
If included at all, a contents list deserves a page of its own. Its headings should be identical to those in the body of the report as this makes them easy to find.

Summary
The summary delivers the report's most interesting points in bite-size chunks. It should briefly set out the report's purpose, main findings, main conclusions and main recommendations. It is designed to give an accurate and rapid understanding of the main issues, enabling busy readers to ignore everything else if they wish. Therefore any main conclusion or recommendation that is qualified elsewhere in the report should also be qualified in the summary. A

summary may contain sub-headings, which should differ from any other main headings in the report.

The summary should mainly be composed of informative not descriptive statements: 'Five staff should be transferred to Section X', not 'A recommendation is made about transferring staff'.

Remember that all your readers will study the summary, whereas perhaps only 30 per cent will read the full report – so allow proper time to prepare it well. In a short report (say, two or three pages), the summary can come after the conclusions and recommendations or be omitted altogether.

If you have written the report well, the summary should be easy to do because it is mainly a cut-and-paste exercise, with some fine-tuning and polishing.

Introduction
The introduction explains the purpose, background, how the work was done and what it cost. It may include brief, simple acknowledgements. Resist the temptation to include key conclusions and recommendations here.

Discussion
(A heading that need not appear if more specific alternatives are available.) The discussion sets out your main results, findings, arguments, options and ideas, preferably under headings and sub-headings so that readers can easily find their way around and skim from point to point. It is likely to be the longest section. See chapter 14 for how to plan it.

Conclusions
Conclusions are inferences you draw from the Discussion, not 'concluding remarks'. It may be more convenient to include them in the Discussion itself but putting them into a separate section may help the reader, especially in a long report.

Recommendations
Your recommendations are the steps you think should be taken, based on the conclusions. Again, it may sometimes be convenient to include them in the Discussion. Recommendations should normally be written in the 'should' or 'should be' style. They can be numbered or bulleted to give them more punch.

Appendices

Any appendices provide a home for fine detail that readers will not need in order to follow the Discussion.

If most readers are unlikely to want the full report, save trees by circulating only a summary with the title and distribution list attached. They can then call for the full report if they wish.

Finally...

Unless you are a novelist, poet or journalist, your writing will rarely be the central delight of a busy reader's day – but then it's not meant to be. Your main aim is to help readers to achieve their objectives which are, to put it bluntly, to Get In, Get On and Get Out. In other words, to access the information readily, progress through it quickly, and stop as soon as possible. Lucid language and structure will help them do so, and that can only be good for your reputation as a clear thinker.

16 | Using alternatives to words, words words

Guideline: *Consider different ways of setting out your information.*

Everyone knows that the written word alone is not always the best way of communicating a message. Graphic devices such as tables, illustrations, pie charts, diagrams, maps, strip cartoons, mathematical formulas and photographs can all help. The difficulty is knowing when to use them and which ones will suit the information. You have to be flexible and experiment a bit to see what works. And, ideally, you should test your decisions with typical readers.

Using tables

An insurance company wants to tell a customer how much her policies are worth, so it uses continuous text:

1/ **You now hold three equity plans. The 2002 plan is mature and is valued at £462.08. The 2003 plan will not become mature until 1 January 2005 and is currently valued at £645.43. The 2004 plan will mature on 1 January 2006 and is currently valued at £438.45.**

These sentences are short and simple enough for any investor who knows that 'mature' means that the policy is ripe for cashing in. (You noticed, though, that the last two sentences switched from negative to positive despite making similar points.) Using elaborate alternatives to text would be unjustifiable for such simple ideas. But a table would be feasible because the information in each sentence consists of a year, a value and a maturity date. Creating a table is fairly easy in most word-processing packages, and might look like this:

2/ You now hold three equity plans, as follows:

Year of plan	Current value	Maturity date
2002	£462.08	Already mature
2003	£645.43	1 January 2005
2004	£438.45	1 January 2006

Or you could try it this way:

3/ You now hold three equity plans, as follows:

	2002 plan	2003 plan	2004 plan
Current value	£462.08	£645.43	£438.45
Maturity date	Already mature	1 Jan 2005	1 Jan 2006

Of the three possibilities, I prefer version 2, as it seems easier to compare the values and maturity dates in vertical columns than in continuous text or rows. The preferred table could be extended easily if, say, details of 10 plans were being given. In continuous text this would be tedious, while you'd need a very wide piece of paper or a wide screen to accommodate 10 tables in the style of version 3.

Exploring other possibilities

The more complex the information, the more the possible choices of presentation multiply, and there is rarely one perfect solution. To show this, here are five ways of presenting the same handful of facts about what a local government department will charge for hiring a hall.

Version 1: *Continuous text: original version*

This version is the real one being used by the department. Though far from total gobbledygook, it doesn't seem clear at first reading:

> Hiring fees of £100.00 or less must be paid in full at the time of booking. In the case of all hiring fees in excess of £100.00 the hirer agrees to pay £100.00 deposit at once on all bookings valued up to £200.00 or 50 per cent of the total hire fee as a deposit on bookings on or over £200.00 in value. The balance of the cost of each hiring must be paid at least 21 days before the date of the event.

I asked several writers to come up with alternatives. Shown below are the four main lines that emerged. In one or two, the tone of voice has changed with the use of 'please' instead of 'must'. (In a contract, 'must' would be necessary.) Otherwise, the content is the same. At the end of all the examples, I'll give the verdict of our focus group. Which do you think is best?

Version 2: *Continuous text: paragraphed version*
This version paragraphs the information:

> If a hiring fee is £100 or less, please pay it in full when you book.
>
> If the hiring fee is from £101 to £199, please pay £100 deposit when you book, then pay the rest at least 21 days before the event.
>
> If the hiring fee is £200 or over, please pay half the hiring fee as a deposit when you book, then pay the rest at least 21 days before the event.

Because the sentence patterns are similar (all beginning with 'if' statements), readers can more easily pick out the details that are relevant to them.

Version 3: *List*
Version 2 could become a list:

> If the hiring fee is:
> - £100 or less, please pay it in full when you book.
> - £101 to £199, please pay £100 deposit when you book, then pay the rest at least 21 days before the event.
> - £200 or over, please pay half the hiring fee as a deposit when you book, then pay the rest at least 21 days before the event.

Version 4: *Questions and answers*

A question-and-answer set-up would also be feasible:

Is the hiring fee £100 or less?
Please pay it in full when you book.

Is the hiring fee £101 to £199?
Please pay £100 deposit when you book, then pay the rest at least 21 days before the event.

Is the hiring fee £200 or over?
Please pay half the hiring fee as a deposit when you book, then pay the rest at least 21 days before the event.

Version 5: *Table*

The final option is a table:

Hiring fee	*Deposit*	*Balance to be paid*
£100 or less	None – pay fee in full on booking	
£101 to £199	£100 deposit, pay on booking	At least 21 days before event
£200 or over	Half hiring fee, pay on booking	At least 21 days before event

The focus group's verdict

The focus group narrowly preferred version 4, giving it an average of 18 points out of 20 for clarity. The differences were small, though: version 5 scored 17; version 3 scored 16; and version 2 scored 15. In terms of first preferences, version 5 was the clear leader: 11 people out of 35 preferred it, while 8 preferred version 4. Version 1 was a distant fifth, scoring 6 points out of 20 for clarity and receiving no first preferences.

These results suggest that the focus group preferred plain English in whatever layout it appeared, but that they regarded layout as an important factor in their ultimate preference between the four plain-English versions. In practice, the best presentation would depend on the document's purpose and the readers' purpose. A question-and-answer layout might be seen as friendlier than a table, but friendliness would be more relevant in a sales leaflet than a legal contract. Readers wanting to get the answers to specific questions might perform better with a table, while those wanting to remember what they had read might perform better with questions and answers.

There are no easy solutions: writers need to know what presentation methods are available, be flexible in using them, and try to find out their readers' reactions to them.

Algorithms

An algorithm may be a good solution if the information aims to help people make a decision from a complicated range of possibilities, or to explain a complicated rule or procedure. Algorithms tend to occupy more space than text and may take a long time to write and lay out, but they can save the readers a great deal of effort. The main danger is that readers may be so put off by the unusual format that they will reject it immediately.

Case history: A charity wanted to gather donations in the most tax-efficient way. It explained several methods, 'Gift Aid', 'Deed of Covenant', 'Payroll Giving' and 'Deposited Covenant'. For simplicity, I haven't included the highly detailed explanations here. The fundraising leaflet said this:

If you pay UK income tax and:

- you want to make a one-off donation of £250 or more, please use Gift Aid;

or - you want to make a one-off donation of less than £250, please use a Deposited Covenant;

or - you want to give regularly and your employer has a payroll giving scheme, please use the scheme;

or - you want to give regularly and your employer does not have a payroll giving scheme, please use a Deed of Covenant.

If you do not pay UK income tax, we will not be able to reclaim tax on your donation but please make a donation anyway.

This seemed easy enough to follow and the charity was satisfied with the level of donations. The next year, however, it decided to put the information into the algorithm shown below. Though other factors may have influenced the result, the charity found that its donations increased by a fifth.

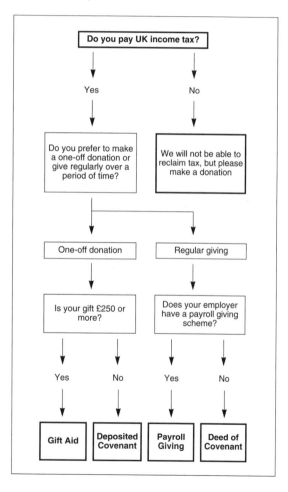

17 | Management of colleagues' writing

Guideline: *Manage colleagues' writing carefully and considerately to boost their morale and effectiveness.*

The managing director of a prominent chain of high-street jewellery shops gave a speech in which he said: 'People ask me how I can sell such attractive decanters so cheaply. And I tell them: "Because they're total crap".'

A plain message, admirably candid, but the wrong message for someone trying to sell jewellery. Within a short time the firm's profits had slumped, he was out of a job, and his name was being removed from the shop-fronts in the chain.

Writers don't usually make such spectacular mistakes in letters to customers, and even if they do, the results are rarely so disastrous. But, over time, the drip, drip, drip of weak writing erodes customer confidence and sullies the image of quality that most managers like to convey. This makes the management of writing an extremely important task that takes care and effort.

One approach is 'hands-off' – not intervening at all in the writing of the staff in the belief that they should take full individual responsibility. Absolute freedom sounds fine in theory but leaves quality to chance – that which is not inspected tends to deteriorate.

Other managers are so hands-on their paw prints are evident on every word. Whatever their staff write is returned with a mass of red-pen amendments, schoolteacher style. This approach may spring from the best of motives – a desire to produce lucid, unstuffy writing – or from a need to show who's in charge. Whatever the reason, the results are the same: managers spend too much time playing editor, and staff become demoralized because they don't know what is wanted or how to improve.

The rest of this chapter tries to chart a middle way.

Working with the team

For the sake of example, let's assume you are managing a team that answers complaints from customers. Though team members deal with many complaints by phone, they also write letters and e-mails. Here are a dozen things you could do.

1   Ask the team how they recognize a good complaint response when they see it. Usually they will agree with you (and me) that the letter should be relevant, accurate, well organized, clear and concise. It should seek to rebuild customer relations and even strengthen them beyond the pre-complaint level.

2   Ask the team what you can do to help them achieve these things. You might be told a few home truths about how you should supervise their writing but you may also get requests for extra training, style guides, books on better English, dictionaries and electronic style checkers.

3   Show one of your own first-draft letters and ask the team to compare it with the final draft you sent. Ask for ideas on how the final draft could have been improved further. Stress that nearly all writing can be improved by the injection of another person's ideas.

4   Show some of the team's letters and ask them to pick out strengths and weaknesses. If there are problems of spelling, punctuation, sense and tone of voice, team members will realize for themselves that they will have to improve. Foster an atmosphere in which writing can be discussed in an unthreatening way. If necessary, bring in a sensitive outsider, such as a writing-skills coach or applied linguist, to take part in the discussion.

5   Discuss the process of writing, particularly the need for planning by writers who use dictation machines or who type or speak directly onto word-processors. Stress that planning will usually save time and raise quality.

6   When you ask a writer to respond to a long or difficult complaint, ask him or her to come back with a detailed plan of the key points. Discuss and agree it before the writer produces a full draft. This will make purpose and content

clear at every step and ensure that the writer follows a clear track from the outset. (Chapter 14 makes some useful points about planning long documents.)

7   Explain what standards you will use to supervise writing. You will be checking for:

- *Purpose*: Is the reason for the letter clear to the reader?
- *Content*: Does the letter contain the right messages and deal with any relevant points the complainant made? Is it accurate, complete and relevant? Is it defensible in the light of your organization's policies or the laws or regulations that govern you? If it is based on a standard letter, has it been tailored appropriately to the individual's circumstances? Does it say what, if anything, the reader should do next?
- *Structure*: Is the material organized in a logical sequence? Does it place the big news early? In a long letter, are headings used to help the reader navigate? If there is an apology, is it positioned early enough? Refer to the various models in chapter 15.
- *Style*: Are the points explained clearly, in sentences of reasonable length with short paragraphs, active-voice verbs, good punctuation and without officialese and business clichés? Is it as warm and friendly as the topic allows?

8   Say that you will try to intervene as little as possible in the writing and that your interventions will seek to make genuine improvements without nitpicking. Your overriding question will be 'Is this letter fit to go?', not 'Is it perfect?' or 'Is it how I would have written it myself?'.

9   Promise that you will explain why, when you make substantial alterations to the drafts your staff provide. This kind of feedback is vital.

10   Make available the tools and information that will help staff to do a good job:

- Buy a good dictionary in book or electronic form.
- Copy and circulate press articles about words.

- Consider asking known good writers in your department to act as coaches and advisers.
- Make your copy of this book available to all. (Or buy several, say the publishers.)
- Add an effective style-checking program to your word-processing software. All style- and grammar-checkers have limitations because they cannot assess the sense, logic or structure of a document, but there are a few good ones. (StyleWriter has been favourably reviewed in the computer press and is used by British and US federal government departments – www.editorsoftware.com)
- For six months or so, circulate letters from each month's output that you think are particularly good. Discuss them at your team meetings.

11 Trust your writers. With proper guidance, they should be able to produce good work without constant supervision. You will still keep an eye on their writing by seeing copies of letters from time to time. Some staff will need more attention than others.

12 Do a survey of recent complainants, including questions about whether they thought the response letters were clear and in the right tone of voice. Commission an annual audit of a sample of your team's letters by a writing-skills consultancy or an applied linguist.

Making the right interventions

Let's consider two examples of writing that should have been substantially improved before they went out.

Case history 1. In the late 1980s, the UK was convulsed by a health scare about fresh eggs. Several people died and there were some 30,000 confirmed cases of food poisoning. The main cause was hens being fed chicken remains and faeces, according to the health minister of the day. One well-known firm of egg distributors (I'll call them Cockerel Brothers) asked hundreds of shop-keepers to reassure their customers by displaying this notice:

Dear Retailer

As a valued customer, for Cockerel Brothers. We would like to assure you of our continual monitering for anything which could affect the quality of our fresh eggs.

Cockerels have just undertook a survey of all our feed mills which involved testing finished feeds and samples (scrappings) from the mills, and having them tested by the Public Health Laboratory. This has resulted in a programme of mill monitering to prevent any bacterial build-up in our mills.

We do not use any raw poultry offal meat, and dried poultry manure in our mills.

We are taking these precautions to endevour our feed is as free from harmful bacteria, as is humanly possible, and manufactured from only wholesome raw materials.

Reassuring, it certainly isn't. There is too much murky detail, and all the errors speak of the kind of carelessness that the notice is warning against, for example:

- The first sentence isn't complete and suggests that the writer is the customer, which would be nonsense.
- 'Undertook' should be 'undertaken', in standard English.
- 'Monitering' should be 'monitoring'.
- 'Endevour' should be 'endeavour'.
- The commas after 'meat' and 'bacteria' are unnecessary.
- It is addressed to the shop-keeper but ought to be addressed to the shopper.
- Implicitly the firm is admitting that harmful bacteria have been allowed to build up in the feed.

No supervisor of writing should have let the notice go out untouched. There should have been a friendly, tactful conversation in which improvements were discussed with the writer so that he or she could rework the text, perhaps trying to emphasize the wholesomeness of the product. It might have said:

Dear Customer
- **Our eggs are fresh and healthy.**
- **We give our hens high-quality food and continually monitor and test it.**

- We do not feed our hens on chicken remains or manure.
- Our priority is to produce eggs that are healthy, wholesome and safe.
- Please contact us on 000 0000 if you would like any further reassurance.

A rival firm in similar circumstances to Cockerel Brothers decided that saying less was a far better way of saying more. Its notice simply said:

EDENDALE EGGS

Healthy Eggs from Healthy Hens.

Case history 2. A housing association is writing to several hundred tenants to explain why modernization work has been delayed. It's an important letter:

BATHROOM MODERNIZATION

First of all apologies for the delay in the start of the bathroom refurbishment programme which was due to start at the end of last year but because the costs came in over budget, further negotiations had to be entered into with the contractors and the extent of the work reconsidered.

Although all the work to the bathroom will be undertaken as previously agreed, we will not be undertaking any work to ground-floor WCs which you may or may not have.

Find attached a draft programme for the anticipated commencement date on your property and we anticipate that the work will take three or four days to complete. Your next contact will be by the contractor, GH Construction, who will contact you individually about a week prior to the start at your house.

If you anticipate any problems with access arrangements or require any further information, please do not hesitate to call Jane Teal on Tameside 99099.

The first question a manager of writing needs to ask is 'Is this fit to go?' My answer would be no. The writer has arranged the points logically and there are plenty of personal words like 'you' and 'we', but officialese, jargon, passives and long sentences are overused.

Great improvement is possible by following good writing tactics. Again you would need to discuss the letter, praise its good points but perhaps show a reworking of the first paragraph as an example of what to do with the rest. It would be useless – and demoralizing to the writer – to redraft the whole letter, though you could provide guidance notes in the margin. Helpful coaching, pleasantly given and co-operatively received, should enable the writer to produce a letter that you would be able to pass as 'fit to go'.

Taking one paragraph at a time, I have underlined possible insertions and shown deletions for the whole letter:

BATHROOM MODERNIZATION

~~First of all apologies~~ I apologize for the delay in ~~the start of~~ the bathroom ~~refurbishment~~ modernization programme which was due to start at the end of last year. ~~but~~ The delay has occurred because the costs ~~came in over budget,~~ were higher than we had budgeted for. ~~further negotiations had to be entered into and~~ We had to negotiate again with the contractors and reconsider how much work we could afford. ~~the extent of the work reconsidered~~.

This splits the long sentence into three and puts the verbs in the active voice.

~~Although all~~ All the work to ~~the~~ your bathroom will be ~~undertaken~~ done as previously agreed~~, we~~. But unfortunately the extra costs mean that if you have a ground-floor toilet, we will not be ~~undertaking~~ able to do any work to ~~ground floor WCs which you may or may not have~~ it.

I have left the first verb in the passive because it will put the stress on 'all the work to your bathroom'. The other changes split the sentence in two and remove the burbling about 'may or may not have'. (It would, of course, be preferable to send one letter to tenants with ground-floor toilets, and a slightly different letter to the rest.)

~~Find attached~~ I attach a ~~draft~~ programme ~~for~~ which shows the ~~anticipated commencement~~ likely starting date for work on your property. ~~and we anticipate that the work~~ We expect the work will take three or four days to complete.

This splits another long sentence and uses plainer English.

~~Your next contact will be by~~ You will hear next from the contractor, GH Construction, who will contact you ~~individually~~ about a week ~~prior to the start~~ before the work at your house begins.

This strengthens the first verb and adds another in place of the noun 'start'.

If you ~~anticipate~~ think the contractor will have any problems with access ~~arrangements~~ to your house, or if you need ~~require~~ any ~~further~~ more information, please ~~not hesitate to~~ call Jane Teal on Tameside 99099.

This costs a few more words in the cause of certainty but also gets rid of waffle. In the final, complete version below, the last sentence has been turned round so that the shorter 'please' clause comes first:

BATHROOM MODERNIZATION

I apologize for the delay in the bathroom modernization programme which was due to begin at the end of last year. The delay has occurred because the costs were higher than we had budgeted for. We have had to negotiate again with the contractors and reconsider the extent of the work.

All the work to your bathroom will be done as previously agreed. But unfortunately the extra costs mean that if you have a ground-floor toilet, we will not be able to do any work to it.

I attach a programme which shows the likely starting date for work on your property. We expect the work will take three or four days to complete.

You will hear next from the contractor, GH Construction, who will contact you about a week before work at your house begins.

Please call Jane Teal on Tameside 99099 if you think the contractor will have any problems with access to your house, or if you need any more information.

The focus group were asked whether they perceived any difference in clarity between this last version and the original.

The average clarity rating was 14 points out of 20 for the original, 17 for the revision. Twenty-five out of 35 people expressed a preference for the revision. The fact that 8 people preferred the original (with two scoring them equal) and that the scores were so close, is a salutary reminder that no-one can please all the people all the time and that audience reaction is rarely uniform. It might even suggest that the letter was fit to send in its original state.

Finally . . .

Criticizing someone's writing can be unnerving for them. So, before you intervene, always consider how you would feel if you were on the receiving end. Remember also that editing is nearly always easier than creating the first draft.

It is fair for you to want a high standard of clarity and grammar from all who write for you. But remember that no two writers will ever use exactly the same words or tone of voice, so trying to impose uniformity will not only be demoralizing but futile.

For those whose writing is criticized, the director-general of the UK's Health and Safety Executive offered this comforting advice in 1988: 'If your draft is rewritten at a higher level, do not despair. Seek to learn from the experience. And bear in mind that a piece of work can be good (and may be appreciated as such), or be very helpful but not usable in its original form.'

18 | Good practice with e-mail

Guideline: *Take as much care with e-mail as you would with the rest of your writing.*

Most of the other guidelines are relevant to e-mail but this chapter offers further points specific to the medium.

Like a paper-based message, an e-mail may be many things: a note to a colleague, a business letter to an external customer or partner, a response to a complaint, or a request for information. It may also become part of an e-mail chain made up of several fragments from different authors.

The main benefits of e-mail are speed, ease of use, and the ability to attach separate documents, photos and illustrations in their precise format from your electronic filing system. The possible drawbacks include:

- responding too hastily or angrily because a reply is so easy to send;
- copying your e-mail to the wrong people, such as a business rival or an opponent in a legal action;
- sending libellous or indiscreet material that others may forward, perhaps to everyone in their address book;
- sending messages that break data protection or obscenity laws;
- copying your message to many people who will have little or no interest in it;
- misjudging the level of formality required and being too friendly or too distant; and
- attaching lengthy documents to your message, just because you can, when these will be irrelevant to most of your readers.

Moreover, because (like me) most e-mail authors have never learned to touch-type and they proofread on the screen (if at all), e-mails tend to contain mistakes that would normally be spotted in a print-out.

These drawbacks need not reduce you to jelly whenever you press 'send', as long as you take reasonable care and follow any 'netiquette' rules your firm imposes.

Planning and structure

The window on screen has an inviting space for typing, so the tendency is to type first and think later. Yet it remains a good idea to plan an e-mail briefly at the outset if you have more than, say, six points to make. Planning helps you collect your thoughts, decide what you really want to say, and in its final stage, use one of the structures in chapter 15 to organize the points. Your most usual structure will be the top-heavy triangle because you will want your main points to be in the immediately visible part of the recipient's screen, answering your reader's inevitable questions:

- 'What's this got to do with me?'
- 'What do you want me to do about it?'

For a lengthy e-mail you can use headings or reduce the length by adding an attachment that has its own system of headings.

At the least, the plan can be a typed list of points on your computer's notepad – put them in no particular order at first; they can be organized later. Alternatively the plan can be a bubble diagram on paper, as shown in chapter 14.

By all means write a first draft at speed based on your plan but let it sit in the 'draft' box for a while, then work on it again. This can help you smooth out the rough edges that can confuse the reader or even cause offence.

Standards

A good heading in the 'subject' line is a good start. It should be specific, reasonably brief and 'predictive' – that is, it should tell the reader what's coming up in the paragraph. So, not 'Proposed meeting' but 'Proposed meeting with Alan Bennett, Gem Design, 22 May, 5pm.' If you are replying to an e-mail, it is courteous to stick to the original heading unless it is obviously wrong. If the e-mail requires an urgent response or is just for information, signal this in the heading. If your e-mail program automatically inserts 'Re' as the first word of the heading, strike a small blow against redundancy by deleting it.

Use a greeting and sign-off. For a formal e-mail that is effectively an external letter, follow letter conventions (chapter 10). So 'Dear Mr Adamson' and 'Yours sincerely', ending with your name, job title, phone number etc (use the automated signature option available in most e-mail programs). Although your e-mail might not appear on your business stationery, it could be printed out by the recipient and circulated as a business letter. An alternative is to prepare a letter in Word or a similar program on your company's electronic letterhead, then attach it to a short covering e-mail.

For a semi-formal e-mail, use the form 'Dear John' or 'John' and 'Kind regards'. For an informal e-mail, you can please yourself but 'Hi John' and 'Regards' are fairly standard forms.

Vary all these possibilities to suit your taste and to comply with company rules. Staff in one British government agency routinely begin their business replies in the form 'Hello Mr Smith'. No-one seems to object, but my preference would be for a more formal start.

Take care to type the salutation correctly. Having complained to an airport about lost baggage, I received an e-mail headed 'Without Prejudice' (a lawyer's way of saying the e-mail couldn't be used in legal proceedings), which then began 'Dear Mr prejudice'.

Though you may have a wide range of fonts, colours, backgrounds and symbols available, be sparing with them unless they will genuinely help to fulfil your purpose. Some recipients' machines may not be able to display all your carefully crafted special effects.

Formality in the text

E-mail seems innately a more informal medium than paper. As we have seen, you need to judge the right degree of formality in the greeting and sign-off, and make similar adjustments in the body of the e-mail. If you are in doubt, err on the side of formality. Sometimes you will want to keep a degree of distance from a customer who is seeking to draw you in to a more informal business relationship than you want. Be aware that others may be reading over the immediate recipient's shoulder. As e-mail is not a particularly secure medium, consider how your message might look on the front page of your local paper. If you are a lawyer, consider how it will sound when read in open court.

Checking carefully

In a note to busy colleagues, occasional spelling mistakes and the like will not cause much dismay as they all make mistakes themselves. But be careful not to be too slipshod, as you will give the impression that you don't care enough about them or the topic to bother getting your words right. And some details do matter – the timing of a meeting, the date of a training course, an amount of money, a missing 'not'. Proofread carefully and slowly – you are not skim-reading for information, but checking for errors.

In this e-mail asking an editor to check a piece of work, the recipient might regard the number of errors as contemptuous of him or her:

Hi. Glad you got the fax. Yes, it's neded asap. Would Friday lunchtime be OK?

I also need to poiht out that it's been through you eagle-eyed editor already – the changes made since then have been tiny, merely gramtaical. Co you need to see the diagrams? If so, I will send them toady.

A second e-mail, requesting a course on proofreading, includes this paragraph:

Our purposes for this course is to increase the speed & accuracy of proof reading. Mistakes can be costly & time consuming, not to mention embarassing for the poof reader! We would like to increase the confidence of the proof readers & provide them with some technikues which would make them less of a labourious task.

So check even your briefest e-mails before sending them off into cyberspace. And be as punctilious with long e-mails as you would with paper-based documents. If necessary, print out your e-mail, polish it on paper, then transfer the amendments to the screen.

Abbreviations and emoticons

Abbreviations are common in informal e-mails. Obvious ones include asap (as soon as possible), wd (would), u (you), pls (please), thnx (thanks), faq (frequently asked question), btw (by the way), fya (for your amusement), fyi (for your information), fwiw (for what it's worth), oic (oh, I see), rec'd (received) and yr (your). In semi-formal or formal e-mails, it is better to avoid using them because some may not be understood and others will seem too casual.

As substitutes for facial expression or body language, emoticons or smileys have enjoyed some popularity but now seem as dated as catch-phrases from the hippy era. The tone of a surly e-mail is scarcely redeemed by a smirking smiley :-) next to the signature. Let the words do the talking, especially in semi-formal and formal e-mails. For informal e-mails, here are a few of the more common smileys:

:-[	sad sarcasm
:-(	sad, angry
;-(	feel like crying
:-&	tongue-tied
:!-(	crying
:-<	very upset
:-*	kiss
;-)	winking
:-#	my lips are sealed
8-O	shocked, amazed

As ever, a sign communicates only if the readers can decode it. If in doubt, write some words.

Inserting your own comments (interpolations)

E-mail enables you to respond by inserting your own comments at various points in the incoming e-mail and returning the whole thing as your reply. If you choose to do this, make clear where your comments start and finish. Using a second colour for your text can work well if it will show up on the recipient's machine. Other good options are indenting your added text, using a markedly different font or enclosing it in square brackets (US, brackets), or some combination of these.

19 | Writing better instructions

Guideline: *Devote special effort to producing lucid and well-organized instructions.*

Everyone has favourite examples of ambiguous instructions:

- On a Marks & Spencer's plastic bag: 'To avoid suffocation keep away from children.'
- On a bottle top: 'Pierce with pin, then push off.'
- On the door of a health centre: 'Family Planning – please use rear entrance.'
- On a hotel breakfast form: 'Please hang outside your room before retiring.'
- In an aircraft maintenance manual: 'Check undercarriage locking pin. If bent, replace.' (The operator examined the pin. It was indeed bent, so he carefully put it back. The aircraft crashed.)
- On a tin of chocolate pudding: 'Before opening, stand in boiling water for ten minutes.'

A lifetime's experience of abysmal product instructions leads many people to read them only when all else fails. Hence the industry slogan 'RTFM' – Read The Flaming Manual. When his car clock failed, a top executive of an American car-maker tried to reset it using the approved company handbook. He couldn't do it. Next day he began a project to rewrite the whole manual in language that a $260,000-a-year corporate captain could understand. Such searing personal experience is often the spur to writing better instructions. Unless some handbook or manual has made you want to disembowel every employee in the company concerned, you might never feel the necessary passion to write it better.

Bad instructions are bad for business. Customers think twice about buying from a company whose instructions have proved useless before. In some countries consumer protection regulations require that instructions and safety information accompanying a product are taken into account when deciding whether it is faulty. Manufacturers can be held liable for injury or damage caused by poor safety information. The selling of unsafe consumer goods can lead to criminal prosecution.

So, what goes wrong in the writing of instructions, and how can problems be put right? Usually some of the following six commandments are broken.

Commandment 1: Remember the readers

Usually readers haven't used the product before, that's why they're reading the instructions. But what else can you find out about them? Will they be technically knowledgeable or complete novices? Will they be children or adults? Under what conditions will they be using the instructions?

Learning about these things and making the right assumptions will affect the words you use. An experienced carpenter might readily understand the instruction 'screw pendant bolts into door plates using cheese-head screws', but most do-it-yourselfers would need an illustration of pendant bolts, door plates and cheese-head screws.

Commandment 2: Favour a simple style of language

This often means using the command form of the verb, known as the imperative:

Switch on the computer

instead of

The computer should be switched on.

By favouring the imperative you are putting the action early and helping to keep the message simple.

Let's say you are instructing office staff how to fill in this box on a computer screen:

New Cost Centre Code	
New Cost Centre Name	
Parent Cost Centre Code	

Using the passive voice you could write:

> The code of the new cost centre should be entered into the New Cost Centre Code field.
>
> The name of the new cost centre (maximum 40 characters) should then be entered into the New Cost Centre Name field.
>
> The code of the parent cost centre should then be entered into the Parent Cost Centre Code field.
>
> When satisfied, the 'Do' key should be pressed to commit the new cost centre to the database.

Or you could write it much more crisply in the imperative:

> Enter the code of the new cost centre into the New Cost Centre Code field.
>
> Enter the name of the new cost centre (maximum 40 characters) into the New Cost Centre Name field.
>
> Enter the code of the parent cost centre into the Parent Cost Centre Code field.
>
> When satisfied, press 'Do' to commit the new cost centre to the database.

This is simpler because the readers know from the start of each sentence what action is required of them. Even simpler would be to assign numbers to the three fields:

New Cost Centre Code	[1]
New Cost Centre Name	[2]
Parent Cost Centre Code	[3]

and then write:

> Enter the correct code in field 1
> Enter the correct name (maximum 40 characters) in field 2

and so on.

Commandment 3: Split the information into chunks

Readers waste time and make mistakes if the information they need is buried in long paragraphs. In this example a local authority inspector is trying to persuade a restaurant owner, whose dirty kitchens she has been visiting, to do his washing-up hygienically. Notice that there are no numbered steps or short paragraphs. The information looks boring and complicated, and you probably don't feel like reading it. That's just what the restaurateur must have thought.

> After the preliminary sorting of the utensils and scraping off of food residues into the refuse containers, the utensils should be washed in the first sink, piece by piece, in clean hot water at a temperature of about 60°C with a detergent added. This temperature is too hot for the hands and the operative should wear rubber gloves and use a dish mop. The water should be changed as often as it becomes dirty or greasy. After this, the utensils should be suitably arranged in the wire baskets available for immersion in the sterilising sink. The utensils should be placed so that no two pieces touch each other and that all the surfaces of every piece are exposed to the rinse water. The rinse will be ineffective if plates or saucers are piled on top of one another or if cutlery is merely heaped in the basket. The sterilising rinse in the second sink should be of clean hot water without added detergent or chemical and at a temperature of not less than 77°C and the utensils should remain in the water for a full two minutes. At this temperature care should of course be taken not to immerse the hands. The purpose is to raise the temperature of the utensils to that of the water so that they will air-dry almost instantly on removal. The temperature of the water should be maintained at about 77°C throughout and accordingly this sink should be fitted with a device to record the temperature of the water. When the two minutes are up, the basket should be removed from the sink and stood temporarily on a draining board and as soon as the utensils are dry and cool enough to be handled, they should be put in a clean place awaiting re-use.

The words are reasonably plain, the punctuation is sound and none of the sentences is impossibly long. But the whole thing needs splitting into short paragraphs ('chunking') and transforming into the imperative. First we need an introductory sentence, perhaps this:

You should make sure that your staff follow these instructions

then the points need redrafting in the imperative:

1 Sort the utensils and scrape off waste food into the bins.

2 Wash the utensils in the first sink, piece by piece, in clean hot water at a temperature of about 60°C with a detergent added. This temperature is too hot for your hands, so wear rubber gloves and use a dish mop.

3 Change the water as often as it becomes dirty or greasy.

4 Put the utensils in the wire baskets available for immersion in the sterilising sink. Arrange the utensils so that no two pieces touch each other and that all the surfaces of every piece are exposed to the rinse water. The rinse will not do its job if plates or saucers are piled on top of one another or if cutlery is merely heaped in the basket. The sterilising rinse should be of clean hot water without added detergent or chemical and at a temperature of at least 77°C.

5 Put the wire baskets containing the utensils in the water for a full two minutes. At this temperature, take care not to immerse your hands. The purpose is to raise the temperature of the utensils to that of the water, so that they will air-dry almost instantly on removal. Maintain the water temperature at about 77°C throughout. To check this, make sure the sink is fitted with a suitable thermometer.

6 When the two minutes are up, remove the basket from the sink and stand it temporarily on a draining board.

7 As soon as the utensils are dry and cool enough to be handled, put them in a clean place awaiting re-use.

These improvements have arisen not from a total rewrite but from two simple structural tactics (chunking and numbering), and one simple style tactic, the use of imperatives.

But are the 'improvements' perceived as such? Yes, according to the focus group. All 35 members preferred the revision. It received an average clarity rating of 18 points out of 20, compared to a generous 10 for the original. The rewrite is still not the finished article: Paragraph 4 needs further work and headings could be used throughout. But it is going in the right direction.

Commandment 4: Use separate headed sections

Normally it is wise to split the instructions into separate sections whose headings identify the purpose of each action.

A common sequence of sections is:

- *Introductory explanation, overview or summary*: This tells readers the purpose of the activity, what it will achieve and how long it should take. Sometimes users with experience of similar tools or equipment will benefit from a quick-start procedure. In long instructions, a contents list will help.
- *Tools or materials required*: Giving this information saves readers from having to stop the job whenever a new tool is needed.
- *Definitions*: These explain any terms the readers may not understand. Definitions may also be needed of everyday words carrying special or limited meanings in the instructions.
- *Warnings*: If these come after the instructions, they are useless and could be dangerous. Warnings should be given twice: once in the introduction and again just before the instruction to which they relate. Make clear that the warnings must be obeyed and are not just recommended practice. Could the product be modified to eliminate the hazard?
- *Main text*, split into headed sections.

The extract opposite from a factory notice shows one way of splitting up text by using headings. Like those in the notice, the headings should be predictive and, if possible, stimulating. Label headings, like 'Spillages' or 'Storage' are weaker than 'What to do about spillages' or 'How much should be stored?'. The other main benefit of headings is that they force the author to group like with like.

Code for use and maintenance of Dominion ink jet printers

Type of substances
Dominion inks use the solvent base methyl ethyl ketone, 'MEK'.
MEK-based inks and solvents are all highly flammable and pose a serious fire and explosion risk if not handled properly.

Is it dangerous to breathe near the vapour?
In normal use there is no health hazard from inhaling the vapour.
If spills are being cleaned up, wear respiratory protective equipment.

Avoiding skin contact
Dominion inks and solvents are not very poisonous but you should still avoid skin contact. If there is a risk of spills or when cleaning up spillages, wear solvent-resistant gloves and goggles.

How much should be stored?
Store as little of these substances as possible in the workroom. Never store more than 50 litres (including waste liquids). Storage should always be in metal cabinets purpose-made for highly flammable liquids.

Clearing up spills
Mop up small spills with industrial wipes or other dry material. After use, put the wipes in a purpose-made fire-resistant lidded bin. Absorb larger spills using a non-combustible material such as sand or Nilflam absorbent. Departments should ensure they have enough materials and equipment to deal with spills.

Dried inks
Deposits of dried ink are highly flammable, so take great care to avoid spills. Clean up dried deposits regularly using non-sparking scrapers. Dispose of the deposits safely.

Use of printers in safe areas
Printers should only be used and maintained in an area free from risk of ignition of flammable vapours. Keep the area well ventilated, particularly at low level. Eliminate sources of ignition such as naked flames and hot elements. Prohibit smoking. Use reduced-sparking tools where possible.

Fire
Suitable extinguishing agents are carbon dioxide, dry powder, alcohol-resistant foam and Halon. Large fires should only be tackled by trained firefighters. If containers get heated, isolate any nearby electrical supply. Then cool the containers by spraying them with water from a safe distance.

Factory notice showing how headings split up the text

Commandment 5: Use appropriate illustrations, labelling and captioning them well

If a message can be simply conveyed in words, there is no need for illustrations (and vice versa). Words are particularly good for getting abstract ideas across, dealing with fine differences in meaning like 'could be' and 'might be', and for referring to things the reader has already learned about. Illustrations are good at showing what things look like and their relative size. This can save words and illuminate the words that remain.

Whether you are commissioning illustrations from graphics professionals or drawing them yourself, you may like to consider such things as:

- using exploded-view format (useful for self-assembly products as they show how the item is put together);
- showing enlargements of particular parts so that readers can focus on the relevant point easily;
- positioning the illustration near the text – ideally readers should be able to refer to it as they read;
- presenting an object at an angle of view that clearly shows the parts concerned or the action to be taken;
- keeping objects to scale;
- ensuring that any typesetting included in the illustration will be legible if scaled down to fit the document.

The instructions opposite for maintaining a pressure cooker lid integrate text and pictures in a straightforward way.

1 Unscrew the indicator cover

2 Remove the indicator and wash it in hot soapy water. Rinse and dry it

3 Unscrew the fixing nut beneath the lid

4 Smear the screw thread with petroleum jelly. Reassemble the parts

Instructions for maintaining a pressure cooker lid

Commandment 6: Test with a panel of typical users

This is the most important commandment, because users' performance is the key. Give the draft instructions, and any product associated with them, to a focus group of typical readers – preferably not your own colleagues who will know too much about the product. Watch them trying to use the instructions. Don't intervene unless asked or unless there is danger. Observe any false moves they make. Discuss with them how they got on. Ask them about any misinterpretations. Redraft the instructions in the light of what you find. Test again if possible.

20 | Lucid legal language

Guideline: *Apply plain-English techniques to legal documents such as insurance policies, car-hire agreements, laws and wills.*

The way many lawyers write is disappointing to their friends and obnoxious to their clients. 'Excrementitious garbage' was how Jeremy Bentham described legal English in the nineteenth century. While every profession tends to cloak its mysteries in unusual language, lawyers have done so more thoroughly than most. But legalese is not sacred. Many lawyers despise it, realize it brings them into disrepute, and are working to remove it. In most English-speaking countries, lawyers campaign for plain language through their umbrella group 'Clarity'. A former chairman, Mark Adler, asks:

> **Why do lawyers write so that no-one can understand them? They say it is because they need to be precise, and that their language has been honed by centuries of litigation. But this is baloney. The real reason is that, although they are paid for their skill with words, most lawyers are dull and clumsy writers who have not broken the bad habits they learnt as students.**

A progressive move came in 1999 when, among other reforms of the civil court system in England and Wales, the Lord Chancellor ordered antiquated Latin and English expressions to be replaced by more modern or exact English. Here is a shortlist of the changes:

Original	*Modern*
Anton Piller order	search order
discovery	disclosure
ex parte	without notice
further and better particulars	requests for information
in camera/in chambers	in private
inter partes	on notice
interrogatories	requests for information
leave of the court	permission of the court

Original	Modern
Mareva injunction	freezing injunction
minor/infant	child
next friend/guardian ad litem	litigation friend
plaintiff	claimant
pleading	statement of case
summons/motion	application
subpoena	witness summons
taxation of costs	assessment of costs
taxing master	costs judge
writ	claim form

Since 2003, the Law Society of England and Wales has required solicitors (under the Solicitors' Charter) to communicate clearly. A similar duty has existed for solicitors in New South Wales, Australia, since 1994. Some of the biggest London law practices describe themselves, with differing degrees of justification, as plain-language firms. They realize that the more international they become, the more customers and colleagues want clarity of expression: legal matters that cross national boundaries are complex enough without language adding to the muddle.

Similarly, organizations that want to win the confidence of customers should give them incomprehensible legal agreements to sign. Now that there are many examples of clear, well-organized insurance policies, credit card conditions and tenancy agreements, it is simply uncompetitive to be locked into legalese.

So the myth is slowly crumbling that obscurity is necessary or part of the price customers are willing to pay. Indeed, with some lawyers charging more for an hour's work than their customers earn in a week, it seems only justice that the writing they provide as part of their service is understandable.

What can be done?

All the techniques described so far in the book can be used to good effect in legal documents. On their own, the techniques will raise the standard of legal writing, though they need to be harnessed to legal knowledge and a genuine care for precision and accuracy.

In the introductory chapter I said that readers needed to be co-operative and well motivated if they were to understand a text in the sense it was meant to be understood. With legal documents, the position is undoubtedly different: some readers will deliberately try to misinterpret a text in their favour. Certainty of meaning is therefore more important. But plain English, cautiously and appropriately used, can make an important contribution to certainty.

It is true that lawyers cannot blithely replace technical legal terms like 'negligence', 'indemnify' and 'estoppel' with one-word equivalents, though they can often provide separate explanations or glossaries. Yet in most legal documents only a few words are genuinely technical. The rest are plain words with ordinary meanings, or legal-flavouring words that smell of the law but can be replaced by plain words or struck out altogether. This spells death, or at best very limited life, for the three ugly brothers 'hereof', 'whereof' and 'thereof', their kissing cousins 'herein', 'hereinafter', and 'hereinbefore' and their wicked uncles 'hereby', 'thereby' and 'whereby'. Such legal flavouring has virtually gone from modern UK laws, which proves how redundant it is elsewhere.

Even if you are not a lawyer, you can play a part in counteracting legalese by questioning its use wherever it appears. You may, for example, be asked to comment on documents written by your own organization's lawyers. Be prepared to comment not just on content but on style and structure. The lawyers may not thank you for invading their territory, but you have something useful to offer – the ability to see the document as non-lawyers will see it.

The clarification of legal documents would make a book of its own, so I want to examine just four proven techniques:

- Replace or cut out legal flavouring.
- Chop up snakes.
- Put people into the writing.
- Add headings.

You will probably have seen worse examples of legal writing than those that follow, but I have chosen them because they are understandable to the general reader while still displaying many of the faults that need to be put right.

Replace or cut out legal flavouring

Case study 1. In this extract from a car-hire agreement, there is legal flavouring and pomposity (underlined):

In the event of car breakdown the owners must at their own expense effect the collection of the car and perform repairs thereto.

The sentence is also ambiguous. I have heard lawyers argue that only the collection would be at the owners' expense, not the repair. But let's assume that both collection and repair are free to the hirer. We can then replace the legalese with plain words. 'In the event of' becomes 'if'; 'thereto' becomes 'to it' or 'to the car'; and 'must effect the collection' becomes 'must collect'. The sentence becomes:

If the car breaks down the owners must collect and repair it, both at their own expense

or

If the car breaks down, the owners must – at their own expense – collect and repair it.

Two points on this:

- The ambiguity of the original has disappeared.
- The revision is shorter. Lawyers used to be paid by the word but now brevity costs them nothing.

Case study 2. A local government department is asking people who apply for a replacement car-parking pass to sign a form. The legal flavouring is underlined:

I hereby declare that the information given above is correct to the best of my knowledge and that I have conducted a thorough search for the said pass and honestly believe that the same cannot be found by me. I agree that in the event of the said pass being found by me I will forthwith return the same to the City Engineer.

All the legal flavouring can safely be removed:

- 'Hereby' just means 'by this writing'.
- 'The said pass' is no more specific than 'the pass' since no other pass is in question. If there were several passes, you would call them 'pass 1', 'pass 2' etc.
- 'The same' is legalese for 'it' or 'them'.
- 'Forthwith' has been given many different interpretations in courts of law – 'immediately' is plainer and would do just as well here.

The legal flavouring doesn't make the form impossible to understand but produces a fusty legal smell whose only purpose is to impress the reader with the solemnity of the procedure. But is it any less solemn in plain English?

I declare that:

- the information given above is correct to the best of my knowledge;
- I have conducted a thorough search for the pass and cannot find it.

I agree that if I find the pass, I will immediately return it to the City Engineer.

Case study 3. Pruning shears are the most appropriate tool when examining this example, in which a city requires a householder to cut back his hedge. Again, the legal flavouring and pomposity are underlined:

<u>Whereas</u> a hedge <u>situate</u> at Dean Road, Moreton belonging to you overhangs the highway known as Dean Road, Moreton <u>aforesaid</u> so as to endanger or obstruct the passage of pedestrians.

<u>Now therefore</u> the Council <u>in pursuance of</u> section 134 of the Highways Act 1959 <u>hereby</u> require you as the owner of the <u>said hedge</u> within fourteen days from the date of service of this notice <u>so to lop or cut the said hedge</u> as to remove the cause of danger or obstruction.

If you <u>fail to comply with</u> this notice the Council may carry out the work required by this notice and may recover from you the expenses reasonably incurred by them in so doing.

If you are aggrieved by the requirement of this notice you may appeal to the magistrates' court <u>holden</u> at Moreton <u>aforesaid</u> within fourteen days from the date of service of this notice on you.

The legal flavouring falls prey to plain words:

- 'Whereas' is fairly common and well understood, but here its use is pointless and creates an incomplete sentence. It can be struck out.
- 'Situate' means 'situated' or 'at'.
- 'Dean Road, Moreton aforesaid' just means 'Dean Road, Moreton'. If there were two Moretons, the correct one would need to be specified by adding the county – 'aforesaid' doesn't aid precision.

- 'Now therefore' is redundant.
- 'In pursuance of' can be replaced by 'under' or 'for the purpose of' or 'using'.
- 'Hereby' is redundant, as it means 'by this writing'.
- 'So to lop or cut the said hedge' just means 'to cut the hedge' or 'to trim the hedge'. *The New Shorter Oxford English Dictionary* says 'lop' means to 'cut off the branches, twigs etc from a tree', so there is no need for both 'cut' and 'lop'. An alternative would be 'cut back'.
- 'Fail to comply with' is a pomposity for 'disobey'.
- 'Incurred' is an unusual though very useful word. For a mass audience, the sentence might need rewriting to remove it.
- 'Holden' is a medieval remnant, meaning 'held'.

With dross swept away and new words underlined, the notice could read:

~~Whereas~~ You are the owner of a hedge ~~situate~~ at Dean Road, Moreton ~~belonging to you~~ which overhangs the highway ~~known as Dean Road, Moreton aforesaid so as to~~, endangering or obstructing ~~the passage of~~ pedestrians.

~~Now therefore the~~ The Council ~~in pursuance of~~, under section 134 of the Highways Act 1959, ~~hereby~~ requires you ~~as the owner of the said hedge~~ within fourteen days from the date of service of this notice ~~so to lop or~~ cut the ~~said~~ hedge, removing ~~as to remove~~ the cause of danger or obstruction.

If you ~~fail to comply with~~ disobey this notice the Council may ~~carry out the work required by this notice~~ choose to cut the hedge and ~~may~~ recover from you ~~the expenses reasonably incurred by them in so~~ its reasonable expenses in doing so.

If you are aggrieved by ~~the requirement of~~ this notice, you may appeal to the magistrates' court ~~holden~~ at Moreton ~~aforesaid~~ within fourteen days from the date of service of this notice on you.

That draft would be fit to show to a lawyer to check for legal accuracy.

The focus group agreed that the revision was much clearer. The 34 who responded gave it an average clarity rating of 18 points out of 20. The original notice averaged only 8. Three police officers in the group, accustomed and perhaps a little loyal to the peculiarities of law language, each gave the original 15 points.

Chop up snakes

Long sentences are another blight in legal documents. Sentences in bank overdraft agreements have been known to stretch to 900 words, monstrosities that show contempt for the readers as well as befuddling them.

This 83-word sentence from an office equipment lease between Bigg, the owner, and Tiny, the company renting the equipment, explains what happens if the equipment breaks down:

> If the equipment shall go out of order, Tiny shall at its own expense have the equipment repaired by the person, firm or body corporate designated by Bigg and in the event of Tiny failing so to do then Bigg shall be entitled to take possession of the equipment and have it repaired at the cost of Tiny and during such possession and repair, the lease charges shall nevertheless accrue and be payable by Tiny to Bigg.

It is obvious that the sentence could be split into three where one part of the story finishes and another begins. This preserves the meaning of the original and all of its word order:

> If the equipment shall go out of order, Tiny shall at its own expense have the equipment repaired by the person, firm or body corporate designated by Bigg~~.~~ ~~and in~~ In the event of Tiny failing so to do then Bigg shall be entitled to take possession of the equipment and have it repaired at the cost of Tiny. ~~and during~~ During such possession and repair, the lease charges shall nevertheless accrue and be payable by Tiny to Bigg.

Then all the shalls could be replaced with 'must' or a verb in the present tense, or both (see chapter 2). Legalese like 'in the event of' and 'nevertheless accrue' could be translated into plain words. The rewrite would say:

> If the equipment goes out of order, Tiny must at its own expense have it repaired by the person, firm or corporate body chosen by Bigg. If Tiny fails to do this, Bigg may take possession of the equipment and have it repaired at Tiny's expense. During such possession and repair, Tiny must still pay the lease charges.

A long sentence is sometimes unavoidable in making a complex point that has exceptions and qualifications attached. Then, it needs to be managed well, with simple construction and plain words. This, for example, in a draft law, is not too bad:

If, in the circumstances of section 3.2 and after the expiry of a 14-day period starting on the date the agreement was entered into, the customer shows by taking some significant action that he considers the agreement to be in force, then:

(a)   the customer may not give the seller notice of cancellation; and

(b)   the seller may enforce the agreement against the customer, despite section 3.2.

Put people into the writing

Most legal agreements are about what people on all sides of a bargain must and must not do. It makes sense to give these people convenient names at the start of the agreement and use them throughout. So 'John Fustian of 97 Sackcloth Court, Berwick' might be identified as 'Fustian', and this term, along with 'he', 'his' and 'him', could be freely used for the sake of brevity. In standard-form agreements it is now common to define the bargain-makers by personal pronouns and this can aid clarity. In an agreement to lease a vehicle, the two sides to the bargain could be defined thus:

'We' means the lessor, Misfit and Snaggs Motors plc, The Garage, Sumpcity.

'You' means the lessee, Paul Oilyhands, 7 Rag Street, Pumptown.

The words 'we', 'you', 'our' and 'your' could then freely be used, improving every sentence in which they appear. It would mean the end of this kind of thing:

The lessor will register details of this lease and the conduct of the lessee's account with any licensed credit reference agency. The lessor may also disclose this and any other information supplied by the lessee to any member or associated company of the Scottish Bank plc group of companies or to any person acting on the lessee's behalf for any purpose connected with the group's business. The lessor may also use the lessee's name and address to mail the lessee about services that may be of interest to the lessee.

Instead it would be possible to write:

We will register details of this lease and the conduct of your account with any licensed credit reference agency. We may disclose this and any other information you supply to any member or associated company of the Scottish Bank plc group of companies or to any person acting on your behalf for any purpose connected with the group's business. We may use your name and address to mail you about services that may interest you.

Add headings

In this deed, lawyers for the local authority involved are trying to rectify a mistake by using highly traditional and legalistic language:

THIS DEED IS MADE the tenth day of January 2001 BETWEEN THE MAYOR AND BURGESSES OF THE LONDON BOROUGH OF BOREHAM of Civic Centre Boreham BU8 2AW (hereinafter called 'the Council') of the one part and Brian Tony Taggart and Miriam Mary Taggart both of 22 Vernon Road Farfield (hereinafter called 'the Purchasers') of the other part.

WHEREAS:–

1)   By a Transfer dated 27 May 1999 and made between the parties hereto the property known as 22 Vernon Road Farfield (hereinafter called 'the Property') was transferred to the Purchasers as therein contained

2)   The said Transfer contains a plan purporting to delineate the property transferred

3)   The said plan does not correctly delineate the property transferred and the plan annexed hereto and marked 'plan No. 2' signed by the parties hereto and dated the tenth day of January 2001 correctly delineates the property

NOW THIS DEED WITNESSETH:–

The said Transfer shall at all times be read and construed as if the plan therein referred to was the said plan No. 2 and not the plan originally annexed thereto but in all other respects the parties hereto confirm the said Transfer

IN WITNESS whereof the Council has caused its Common Seal to be hereunto affixed and the Purchasers have set their hands and seals the day and year first above written

The points are not very complicated. There was a mistake in the plan attached to the original transfer documents. The parties want to put this right by attaching a new plan. So Mr and Mrs Taggart would probably like a clearly written document they can take out of their files in a few years' time and understand immediately without going to a lawyer.

By grouping the information carefully under headings, this should be possible. Little legal flavouring is needed. As long as the document is signed as a deed and witnessed properly, it will have legal effect. A possible transformation into plain language would say:

Deed of Amendment

Date

10 January 2001

Parties

1   London Borough of Boreham, Civic Centre, Boreham BU8 2AW ('the council').

2   Brian Tony Taggart and Miriam Mary Taggart, both of 22 Vernon Road, Farfield ('the buyers').

Property

22 Vernon Road, Farfield ('the property').

Background

1   By a transfer dated 27 May 1999 between the parties, the property was transferred to the buyers.

2   The transfer contained a plan ('Plan 1') that showed the property incorrectly. A second plan attached to this deed ('Plan 2') correctly shows the property. It was signed as correct by the parties on 10 January 2001.

Outcome

The transfer is to be read as if Plan 2 and not Plan 1 had been attached to it. In all other respects, the parties confirm the transfer.

Signatures

Signed as a deed on 10 January 2001:

• by the council's authorized officer –
• by the buyers –

Witness to the buyers' signature –

Though this is only a short example, its use of headings and simple style can be applied when much more complex matters have to be expressed in legal terms.

21 | Basics of clear layout

Guideline: *Use clear layout to present your plain words in an easily accessible way.*

Plain English needs to be complemented by effective layout otherwise only half the job has been done. At its simplest, in a letter or short report, effective layout might mean using easily legible type and putting ample space between paragraphs. At its most complex, in instructions, detailed official forms or web pages, effective layout might require the manipulation of hundreds of variables such as different typefaces, headings of various sizes, colours, and illustrations.

Not so long ago, layout was largely outside writers' control. Typesetting was an expensive mystery guarded by layout professionals. Now, with the advent of desk-top publishing (DTP) and web-design software, many writers have access to sophisticated layout tools. But if these tools are not used with a reasonable degree of skill, if there is no sense of what makes a page look good, or if readers' strategies for tackling a document are ignored, then the results can be dire – poor layout can negate many of the benefits of plain English.

There is no simple recipe book for good layout, but this chapter summarizes key points that you may like to bear in mind when preparing a layout or getting others to do so. Naturally, for important or high-use documents, you may need help from layout and printing professionals who have undergone rigorous typographical training.

Some of the guidance here is more appropriate to the highly flexible DTP and Web environments than to word processing, though these fields increasingly overlap. The points are intended to supplement the technical guidance that software manuals tend to cover. For simplicity I have set out the points in question-and-answer form.

What is the best way to get a feel for good layout?

Study layout critically – books, reports, letters, website texts, forms, and your car and life insurance policies. Every line of type on every page or website, every ruled line and every white space is the result of someone's conscious layout decision, for good or ill. The sum of those decisions is what gives a page its distinctive look. By going through the document yourself – say by filling in a form – you can see whether it is usable as well as legible.

Consider which documents are easy on the eye, and why? Which organize the material well, and how do they do this? Economy is often an important factor, so if a large number of words has been squeezed into a page, what has been done (or not done) to make the result easily legible?

Consider how different layouts fulfil different purposes – to attract attention, to sell, to summarize main points, to ask questions, to act as reference material, to save space. Consider whether the layout styles fulfil their purposes.

In paper documents, what is a good page size to use?

This depends on many things such as the amount of information, how the readers use the document (do they need, for instance, to carry it around with them on a building site or to follow a route?), whether it is to be stored and filed, or whether it needs to be fed through photocopiers or laser printers.

In Europe the commonest range of sizes – and therefore the most economical – are the 'A' sizes such as A3 (297×420 mm), A4 (210×297 mm) and A5 (148×210 mm). Each of these is formed by folding in half, along the long edge, the next biggest 'A' size. All the sizes offer an infinite number of layout possibilities. Most business letterheadings are A4, and a single column of type is the obvious layout choice. But an information leaflet might have two columns to the A4 page and be double-sided; this allows a great number of words to be fitted in. An A4 page could be divided into one narrow column (perhaps for side-headings) and one wide column for the associated main text. Many leaflets are A4 folded twice on the long edge, producing a 6-panel set-up – one panel for a front cover, perhaps, and five for other information.

The 'B' sizes offer other interesting possibilities, especially when you want to create a distinctive look to your sales literature. B4 is 250 × 353 mm, B5 is 176 × 250 mm, and B6 is 125 × 176 mm.

In the US, common sheet sizes are 25 × 38 in, 26 × 40 in and 36 × 48 in, from which the sizes for booklets, leaflets, etc. can be derived. Common sizes for trimmed stationery are 8.5 × 11 in, 8.5 × 14 in (US legal) and 7.5 × 10 in.

What are the key variables to control for high legibility?

Three important variables are type size, column width and space between lines ('leading', pronounced 'ledding'). These interact in ways that improve or impair legibility. While it is impossible to lay down rules for how these variables should be manipulated, some guidelines may help.

Type size: Type size is measured from just above the top of the capitals to just below the bottom of letters like y and j. The distance can be measured in points. (A point is about 1/72 inch.)

In many typefaces the sizes 9-point and above will be highly legible for large areas of continuous text on paper, though this will depend on how the other variables are handled. On web pages, a bigger size will be needed if the text is to be read on screen.

Point size alone is an uncertain guide to how big the type appears to be. Here are examples of 10-point type in two typefaces, Monotype Bembo and Monotype Nimrod ('typeface' means a set of lettering in a certain design):

Example of 10-pt Monotype Bembo, a widely available typeface based on a fifteenth-century Italian type.

Example of 10-pt Monotype Nimrod, designed in the 1970s for newspaper text setting.

Though both are 10-point, the characteristics of Nimrod make it appear bigger than Bembo. This is mainly because in Nimrod the x-height (height of the lower case *x*, *o*, *m*, *n*, etc) is great in proportion to the type size. So x-height is a better guide to legibility than point size. Provided the x-height is 1.5 mm or more, printed type will be highly legible to those with normal eyesight under good reading conditions. For a mass audience, though, 1.8 mm is more reasonable. Documents to be read from a distance – posters, say – will need a bigger type size. In a reference document you might be content to use a small point size, say 7-point, for the sake of economy – but you would choose a typeface whose x-height was large enough to make the point size reasonably legible and you would use narrow columns.

If some of the audience are known to have poor eyesight, an x-height of at least 3 mm is appropriate. An alternative is to offer large-print and Braille versions of documents. Websites can be adapted in various ways to accommodate the needs of visually impaired people – your website designer should be able to advise on the latest possibilities.

Column width: For large areas of text on paper, most layout professionals reckon that the optimum column width is 50–70 letters and spaces. This means about 8 to 12 words per line, as in the column width you are reading now. In research with a sample of 4,000 people, Colin Wheildon found that 38 per cent thought text was hard to read if the lines extended beyond 60 characters.

Certainly a common mistake is to set small type across too wide a column, such as 170 mm on an A4 page. The result could be more than 100 letters and spaces to the line unless the type is correspondingly big. And if the type is big, there will be fewer words to the page so printing or copying costs could increase.

Leading: Normally there needs to be some leading, otherwise readers tire easily and make mistakes when locating the start of successive lines. The amount of leading depends on the trade-off you make between economy and legibility. As a guide, try to ensure that the leading is about a fifth of the type size. So 12-point type might benefit from leading at 2.5 or 3 points. Generally, the wider the column, the more leading is needed. Typefaces with a large x-height relative to their type size (like most versions of Times, Helvetica, Arial, Plantin and Palatino) tend to need the full allowance of leading; those with a smaller x-height (like Futura, Bodoni and Bembo) tend to need less.

So which is the best typeface to use for high legibility?

What works well in one set of circumstances may not work well in another. Generally, the type for printed body text should be quiet, simple and regular in form without the eccentricities of display typefaces such as those on the fascias of hamburger joints or on advertising hoardings. For large areas of printed text, it is usually better to use a serif type (that is, a type with tiny strokes or projections at the end of most of the letters). The serifs guide the eye horizontally and put light and shade on the page because the letters have thick and thin strokes. Serif types tend to look rather more authoritative, classical and official. The text type in this book is a serif, the Monotype version of Plantin.

Highly legible serif types include Plantin, ITC Garamond, Joanna, Century Schoolbook, Palatino and Times. These are their industry names; trade names may differ for commercial or copyright reasons.

Example of a version of Joanna, set in 10-point. It has a distinctive *italic* face, and a good **bold** weight too.

Example of Century Schoolbook, again in 10-point. The *italic* face may not be very pleasing, but the **bold** type is strong and effective.

Example of Palatino, set in 10-point type. In this there is a distinctive *italic* type and a good **bold** weight.

Times is available in most DTP and word-processing software, but its narrow character width tends to make it more suitable for newspaper columns. Its universality makes it an unusual choice for any layout professionals who want to create an individual look for their client's documents. In short, it is a little boring.

The sans-serif types (types without serifs) tend to be more useful as headings and in forms, catalogues and flyers, though they can look good in almost any application if handled well. They have enjoyed a resurgence on websites as they seem easy to read on screen. Sans faces tend to be plain, unfussy and very compact, so in bold weights they make an especially strong impact. Good sans faces include Helvetica, Gill, Franklin Gothic and Frutiger. The Arial font, which is similar to Helvetica, is now as common as Times.

A modern version of Gill which, like Joanna, was cut by the English artist Eric Gill. This is 10-point Gill Light, with *italics*. **This is the bold weight.**

Example of Franklin Gothic, also in 10-point but with a powerful bold weight.

Example of Frutiger in 10-point, with an effective **bold weight**. The type was designed by Adrian Frutiger.

Many documents combine sans-serif type for headings with serif type for body text. The opposite combination is less common but can still work well.

What about ways of emphasizing type?

Most typefaces can be used in weights such as roman (this weight), bold, italic and bold italic. A popular type like Helvetica has as many as 28 weights. In a single document, it is usually better to use as few weights as are really necessary and to make sure there is ample difference in strength between them. In some typefaces, especially sans faces, the italic weight is merely a sloping version of the roman and may not be noticeably different, especially on website pages.

Use highlighting weights sparingly – if you emphasize too much, nothing will be emphasized. If too many individual words are typed in bold, pages will look spotty or dazzling and the reader will find concentration difficult.

Most people with normal eyesight dislike reading long swathes of bold, italics, and capitals. Of these, capitals tend to be the most disruptive to reading and may seem aggressive. There is no harm in capitalizing a few words, but the usual mix of upper and lower case is the best for legibility. There is no need to set headings in capitals; generally they will look better in upper and lower case.

In typewriting, underlining was one of the few available ways of emphasizing text. The weight of rule corresponded to the weight of the type and the effect was pleasant enough in small doses. In DTP, underlining is probably the least attractive way because the line will usually <u>slice through the bottom of the type unpleasantly</u>, like this. Only do it if there's no other way.

Any hints on the use of white space?

Without wasting paper unnecessarily, you should allow generous margins and reasonable space between columns. Resist the temptation to fill white space with type. The same point applies to website pages. It is no tragedy if a section of a report ends halfway down a page or if the back of a leaflet has to be left blank.

If you are leaving space between paragraphs (a common alternative to indenting the first line), ensure the space adequately separates one paragraph from the next but don't allow the paragraphs to look like islands. The software will generally allow you to set up style-sheets to exert fine control over inter-paragraph space.

If headings appear in a column of text, be sure to put at least as much space above them as below them, otherwise they will appear to be floating upwards to the previous paragraph.

If there are bullets, don't indent them excessively (or even at all), and don't unduly separate the text from them – 5 mm is enough.

Is it a good idea to reverse out the type?

Reversing out means printing the type in white out of a background colour. Usually this will only be highly legible if the type is at least 10-point in a bold weight and if the background colour is dark. Sans-serif faces tend to reverse out better than serif. Only reverse out small areas of type.

Should type be printed on a coloured background?

Not if it destroys the clarity of the type. For most purposes, there needs to be strong contrast between foreground (the type) and background. If you use dark green type on a pale green background, you are asking for trouble, especially as about eight per cent of males are colour blind for green and red and may see these colours as grey.

Is it a good idea to track or scale the type?

Tracking means adding or taking out space between letters. In this paragraph I have added extra units of tracking, with obviously unpleasant results. There comes a point when excessive tracking disrupts the readers to the extent that they start to look at individual letters instead of reading words by their shape and in sweeps of four or five words at a time.

In this paragraph, I have deducted several units of tracking, producing an equally foul outcome. If done at all, tracking needs to be sensitive and to respect the design characteristics of the typeface.

Similar points apply to the ability of some software to scale the type to compress or expand it. Don't overdo this: be sensitive to the design of the typeface and to your readers' eyesight.

The term 'hierarchy of headings' is often used. What does it mean?

A document may need to use several sizes or weights of heading to signify, for example, chapter headings, sub-headings and paragraph headings. This range of sizes or weights (or both) is the hierarchy of headings. In general, the strength and position of headings should reflect the job they are being asked to do. So chapter headings will usually be considerably stronger than sub-headings, which will in turn be stronger than paragraph headings. This is similar to the arrangement used in this book. The hierarchy of headings should be applied consistently – readers get confused if the same signal is used with different meanings.

Should I use justified type?

Justification means inserting spaces between words (and even between letters) so that all the lines of type take up the full column width. Hyphenation at line-ends may also be needed to make this work. The main reasons for justification are economy and, according to some, greater neatness.

There is no clear-cut evidence that competent justification impairs the reading performance of literate adults. Sometimes, though, mechanical justification tends to produce rivers of white space running down the text as well as very uneven letter-spacing. If you dislike the justified type your machine produces, your software manual may offer help. For example, you should be able to adjust the program so that it applies line-end hyphenation only to words of seven letters or more and so that it bars more than two successive line-end hyphenations.

Unjustified type ('ranged left' or 'flush left') tends to produce a more relaxed, informal look. Word-spacing remains constant. The hyphenation program can be switched off if you dislike line-end hyphenation, though the drawback is a more ragged right-hand edge to the column. With unjustified type you will want to avoid breaking up the left-hand edge of the column by excessive indentation. In this case, try to use the left-hand edge as the starting point for as much of the material as possible.

By editing or other adjustments, try to remove widows (single words forming the last line of a paragraph), especially if they appear as the first line of a page. They waste space and look unsightly. This applies equally to justified and unjustified type.

Does the use of colour help?

Cost normally prohibits the use of a second colour (or several colours) on anything except pre-printed stationery, external publications with long print-runs, and websites. But if colours are available, do not spatter them throughout the text. Use them mainly to help people navigate through the document, perhaps by applying the same colour to all headings or to one level of heading. Use colour also to add impact, say on a front cover. In forms, a second colour is now common (perhaps as a percentage tint) to surround white completion boxes; this helps them to stand out.

What paper should I use?

This depends on your budget and the conditions under which the document will be used. If possible, take advice from a printing professional. Heavy, gloss papers tend to be expensive and may make the type hard to read in certain lighting conditions. Thin papers create an unacceptable amount of show-through when printed on both sides. Certain weights and finishes are treated unkindly by photocopiers and laser printers. Papers with a high recycled waste content are gradually improving in quality and in their range of weights, finishes and colours.

Doesn't decent layout cost more?

The work has to be done, so it might as well be done properly. A poorly laid out form, for example, may substantially impair readers' performance and this adds to administrative costs if it has to be returned for re-completion. Government departments reckon that the cost of laying out and printing a form is as little as half of one per cent of the cost of administering it after completion. A life insur-

ance policy might cost 20p (US 40c) to print, yet the first year's pre-
miums could easily be a thousand times that. So good layout is
unlikely to add significantly to costs.

To showcase most kinds of essential information, nothing more
than decent competence is needed in the layout. Often the best
results come from quiet, unshowy pages that the readers hardly
notice. There's no need to shout. Colin Wheildon says,
'Typography must be clear. At its best, it is virtually invisible.'
Similarly, harmonious-looking websites (preferably with links that
work) are likely to maintain readers' interest better than sites that
are all show and noise.

The next four pages show layout features in two documents.

Page from a form, showing a hierarchy of heads and vertical spaces

Paragraph heads are nearer to the text below them than above them, while spaces between paragraphs are greater than those between sub-paragraphs. Line length is about 75 characters, which is a shade too long. The background is 10 per cent black; in practical use a pale pastel would be better. The column is offset slightly – more energetic than centring.

Renewal form for
Council Tax Benefit and Housing Benefit

Ref no   Date issued

Name
Address

Postcode

Who this form is for
This form is for people who are getting Council Tax Benefit or Housing Benefit now. You can use it to renew one or both of these benefits.

Filling in the form
You must answer every section in the form, otherwise it will take us longer to work out your benefit.

Don't forget to sign at the end of the form. If you have a partner, he or she must sign the form as well. (Partner means someone you are married to, or someone you live with as if you are married to them.)

We will treat anything you tell us as confidential.

After you have filled in the form
When you have filled in the form, send it back to us straight away. Then, if you are still allowed benefit, we will carry on paying it to you without a break.

If you do not send us the form, or there is a delay, you may lose benefit. This usually means you will have to pay more Council Tax or rent.

After we have worked out your benefit
After working out your benefit we will send you a letter saying how much you will get. If your Council Tax Benefit has changed, we will also send you a bill for the new amount.

If you cannot get benefit
If we cannot renew your benefit, we will write and tell you why. The letter will tell you how to appeal if you think our decision is wrong.

please turn over

Second page of the form

This continues the layout themes of the first page. The wide left-hand margin makes room for navigational markers like 'Part A'. Question numbers hang outside the wide column in their own space; they are also picked out in bold. At full size, the answer spaces are about 8 mm deep, adequate for normal handwriting. It's a very spacious layout. Notice that the boxes for 'yes' and 'no' put 'no' first. This is more logical as the people who answer 'no' can be shunted elsewhere immediately.

Part A About you

1 What is your surname?

2 What are your first names?

3 What is your title? *(for example Mr, Mrs or Miss)*

4 What is your date of birth?

/   /

5 What is your National Insurance number? *(if you know it)*

6 What is your daytime telephone number, if you have one? *(You do not need to tell us, but it might speed up your claim if we need to contact you.)*

Part B About your partner

1 Do you have a partner who normally lives with you?
No ☐ Go to **Part C**
Yes ☐

2 What is your partner's surname?

3 What are your partner's first names?

4 What is your partner's title? *(for example Mr, Mrs or Miss)*

5 What is your partner's date of birth?

/   /

6 What is your partner's National Insurance number? *(if you know it)*

7 Is your partner registered blind?
No ☐
Yes ☐

2

Page from a debt advice booklet, designed by the author
This introduces the booklet's principal topics with two main headings and a bullet-point list. As this is the first left-hand page of the booklet, there is no sense in filling it with text – right-hand pages are likely to be examined more thoroughly. The page benefits from a jaunty graphic which emphasizes that advice is only a phone call away.

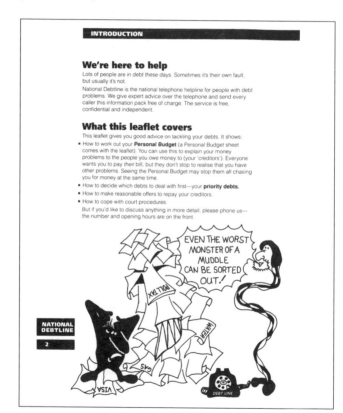

INTRODUCTION

We're here to help
Lots of people are in debt these days. Sometimes it's their own fault, but usually it's not.

National Debtline is the national telephone helpline for people with debt problems. We give expert advice over the telephone and send every caller this information pack free of charge. The service is free, confidential and independent.

What this leaflet covers
This leaflet gives you good advice on tackling your debts. It shows:

- How to work out your **Personal Budget** (a Personal Budget sheet comes with the leaflet). You can use this to explain your money problems to the people you owe money to (your 'creditors'). Everyone wants you to pay *their* bill, but they don't stop to realise that you have other problems. Seeing the Personal Budget may stop them all chasing you for money at the same time.
- How to decide which debts to deal with first—your **priority debts.**
- How to make reasonable offers to repay your creditors.
- How to cope with court procedures.

  But if you'd like to discuss anything in more detail, please phone us— the number and opening hours are on the front.

EVEN THE WORST MONSTER OF A MUDDLE CAN BE SORTED OUT!

NATIONAL DEBTLINE

2

DEBT LINE

Same booklet, later right-hand page

This two-column layout enables plenty of text to be included in an A4 page, while still remaining easy on the eye. In the published version, headings were printed in green with the rest of the type in black. The column width allowed about 45 letters and spaces to the line.

MORTGAGE ARREARS

Mortgage arrears

You may have both first and second mortgages.

The **first mortgage** is the loan you took out to buy your home.

The **second mortgage**, also known as a *secured loan*, *second charge* or sometimes a *consolidated loan plan*, is a separate loan which is secured on your home.

Check all your loan agreements to see if they are 'unsecured' or 'secured' on your home. If 'secured' treat them as priority debts because lenders can ask the court for possession of your home if you cannot pay your monthly instalments. The property can then be sold to pay off your debt.

The legal term for the company or building society who gave you your mortgage is a 'mortgagee'. In this leaflet we call them 'lenders'.

Contact your lenders if you have problems

It's never too early or too late.

You may not be in arrears yet or your lenders may have started court action. Whatever the situation, **do not delay** contacting your lenders. Get in touch as soon as possible by writing, phoning or making an appointment to see them. If the local office is unhelpful or difficult, contact their head office and try to reach an agreement with them.

If you have not paid the mortgage for a number of months it's very important that you start paying what you can, even if this is not the full monthly payment.

Arranging to clear the arrears

> **Warning**
>
> Don't be tempted to take out an extra loan to repay your mortgage arrears. Often these are very expensive and could put your home at greater risk.

You will usually have to offer an extra monthly payment to clear the arrears. The lenders will normally ask for the arrears to be cleared over 12 to 24 months. But even longer periods can be agreed in some circumstances. If you cannot manage to clear the arrears within the time the lenders want, start paying the amount you have offered anyway. Explain why you can't pay the amount they have asked for, particularly if there are circumstances such as a long illness, death of a partner, marriage breakdown or unemployment.

If the value of your home is far more than the total mortgage, tell the lenders. The more your house

is worth, the less risk your lenders are taking.

If your home is not worth as much as the mortgage, see the section on page 10.

Sometimes your lenders may be able to accept another arrangement. We describe some of them below.

Adding the arrears to your mortgage

This is called 'capitalising' the arrears.

Normally you can only do this:

- on first mortgage arrears; and
- if the value of your property is a lot more than the total amount of your mortgage.

It works like this: the amount of the arrears is added to the total mortgage. The monthly repayments are increased to take account of this. So the arrears are spread over the remaining years of the mortgage term.

Your lenders may be more likely to agree to this if you have already kept to a payment agreement for some months—it shows you are able to pay.

Changing to a repayment mortgage

If you have an endowment mortgage you may be able to change this to a repayment mortgage. Endowment mortgages include an insurance policy and if you have had this policy for a few years it may have a surrender value. The surrender value is the amount of cash the policy is worth if you cancel it.

Ask your lenders about this and get advice on whether:

- it is a good idea to cash in your endowment policy;
- changing to a repayment mortgage will reduce your monthly payments.

If you cancel your endowment policy, ask your lenders about a mortgage protection policy. This would cover the payments if you died.

If you do change to a repayment mortgage you should also ask your lenders to extend the mortgage term to 25 years. (See below.)

Increasing the mortgage term

Most mortgages are spread over 25 years — this is called the mortgage term. If you have already lived in your home for several years, you could ask your lenders to extend the term back to 25 or even 30 years. This could cut the regular monthly payment so that you can afford to pay something towards the arrears each month. If you have an endowment mortgage, this may be more difficult. Ask your lenders.

NATIONAL
DEBTLINE

9

| *Sources and notes*

General sources

Butcher J *Copy-editing* (Cambridge 1992).

Carey G V *Mind the Stop* (London 1958).

Eagleson R D *Writing in Plain English* (Canberra 1990).

Felker D B and others *Guidelines for Document Designers* (American Institutes for Research 1981).

Gowers E *The Complete Plain Words* (London 1986).

Greenbaum S *An Introduction to English Grammar* (Harlow 1991).

Hart's Rules for Compositors and Readers (Oxford 1983).

Howard G *The Good English Guide* (London 1993).

Miller C and Swift K *The Handbook of Non-Sexist Writing* (London 1989).

Swan M *Practical English Usage* (Oxford 1993).

Truss L *Eats, Shoots and Leaves* (London 2003).

Turk C and Kirkman J *Effective Writing* (London 1989).

Williams J M *Style* (Glenview, Illinois 1981).

Legal language

Adler M *Clarity for Lawyers* (London 1990).

Asprey M M *Plain Language for Lawyers* (Sydney 2003).

Charrow V R and Erhardt M K *Clear and Effective Legal Writing* (Boston 1986).

Cutts M and Wagner E *Clarifying EC Regulations* (Stockport 2002). Available free online from www.clearest.co.uk

Cutts M *Lucid Law* (Stockport 2000).

Garner B A *Dictionary of Modern Legal Usage* (Oxford 1987).

Kimble J *Answering the Critics of Plain Language* The Scribes Journal of Legal Writing, 1994-95 Vol 5.

Mellinkoff D *The Language of the Law* (Boston 1963).

Wydick R *Plain English for Lawyers* (Durham, N Carolina 1985).

Specific sources and notes

Starting points

page 5 For the development of plain English, see the *Oxford Companion to the English Language*, edited by Tom McArthur (Oxford 1992).

page 6 The remarks of Coode and Bentham are quoted in *Writing Rules: Structure and Style*, an unpublished paper given by David C Elliott to the International Conference on Legal Language at the Aarhus School of Business, 1994.

page 9 The Associated Press report was carried by the *Sacramento Bee*, 14 January 1997.

page 12 The booklet *Health and Safety at Motor Sports Events* (HGS112) is available from HSE Publications.

page 14 Current activities of plain-language practitioners worldwide are to be found via the website of Plain Language Association International, www.plainlanguagenetwork.org

page 15 The studies on jury instructions are quoted in Joseph Kimble's paper *Answering the Critics of Plain Language* (cited above). The primary sources are Charrow R P and Charrow V R *Making Legal Language Understandable: A Psychological Study of Jury Instructions*, 79 Columbia Law Review 1306, 1370 (1979); and Benson R W *The End of Legalese: The Game Is Over*, 13 New York University Review of Law & Social Change 519, 546 (1984–85).

page 15 Work on the SSA form is thoroughly described in *Clarity*, issue 45 pp 2–4, www.clarity-international.net

page 15 Work on the Clearer Timeshare Act is published in Cutts, *Lucid Law* (cited above). This and other efforts to clarify statutes are explored in *The Law-Making Process* by Michael Zander (London 1994).

chapter 1

page 20 The analysis of American sentence length is included in *Computer Analysis of Present-Day American English* by Kucera H and Francis W N (Providence, Rhode Island 1967).

chapter 2

page 36 The study referring to unconsciousness was reported in *The Daily Telegraph* on 24 February 2000.

page 37 The research study among scientists is described in Turk and Kirkman, cited above.

chapter 3

page 54 Strunk is quoted in *The Elements of Style* by Strunk W and White E B (New York 1979).

chapter 4

page 61 Orwell's prescriptions are quoted under his entry in the *Oxford Companion to the English Language* (cited above) and in his essay *Politics and the English Language*, included in *Shooting the Elephant and Other Essays* (London 1950).

page 67 Among those who recommend the use of 'I' and 'we' are Booth V *Writing a Scientific Paper* (London and Colchester, The Biochemical Society 1981); Sandman P M and others *Scientific and Technical Writing* (CBS College Publishing 1985); and Barrass R *Scientists Must Write* (London 1978).

page 69 Information on the passive percentage is drawn from a manual accompanying the software program *StyleWriter – the Plain English Editor* (Editor Software Pty Ltd 1994).

chapter 11

page 98 The role of punctuation in showing the construction of the sentence is described in *Mind the Stop* (cited above) and in *Eats, Shoots and Leaves* (cited above).

page 101 My dislike of the 'nameless thing' is shared by *Hart's Rules*, cited above.

chapter 12

page 115 Nesfield's book, long out of print, was published by Macmillan, London.

page 119 A detailed study of readability formulas is given in *Predicting Readability of Data Processing Written Materials* by Ronald Guillemette (Data Base, summer 1987, pp 40–47). Another useful source is *Tackling NHS Jargon* by Sarah Carr (Abingdon 2002).

chapter 14

page 126 The core statement is a variation of the core sentence described in *Write To Win* by Thomas McKeown (Clear Communications Press, North Vancouver 1987).

page 129 For the section on different approaches to planning, I have drawn upon *Writing Strategies and Writers' Tools* by Daniel Chandler (*English Today* 34, Vol 9, 2 1994).

page 130 Dr Flowers' work is reported in *Getting the Structure Right: Process, Paradigm and Persistence* by Christopher Balmford, *Clarity* 43 pp 14–23, May 1999. The original source is *Madman, Architect, Carpenter, Judge: Roles and the Writing Process*, 44 Proceedings of the Conference of College Teachers of English 7–10 (1997).

chapter 16

page 147 The use of algorithms, flow charts and other alternatives to continuous prose is thoroughly described in James Hartley's *Designing Instructional Text* (London 1991). Another excellent source is Doris Wheatley's *Good Business Communication* (London 1988).

chapter 20

page 172 Mark Adler was writing in the *Information Design Journal* 7/2 (1993): *Why Do Lawyers Talk Funny?*

chapter 21

page 185 Colin Wheildon's work is described in *Type and Layout: How typography and design can get your message across – or get in the way* (Strathmore Press Inc, Berkeley, California 1995).

Index